# The Abiding Church

Creating, Cultivating, and Stewarding a Culture of
Discipleship

## Nate Sweeney

**Sermon To Book**
**www.sermontobook.com**

**The Abiding Church / Nate Sweeney**
ISBN-13: 978-1-945793-50-9
ISBN-10: 1-945793-50-3

*A special thank you to my best friend and biggest fan—
my wife, Monica.*

*You have seen the best and worst of me and love both. You
have always encouraged me to walk in personal abandonment
and absolute trust in Christ no matter what that meant. I love
you and appreciate you more than you could ever know.*

*Thanks, Babe!*

# CONTENTS

# Dear Church Leader

We have, somehow, got hold of the idea that error is only that which is outrageously wrong; and we do not seem to understand that the most dangerous person of all is the one who does not emphasize the right things.[1]
**—D. Martin Lloyd-Jones**

This book is written from my heart to yours as a fellow laborer in the ministry. I look at the calling that God has placed on my life as a sacred responsibility, as I am sure you do, also. My desire is not to teach some new revelation or to unpack some deep truth that has yet to be discovered. Rather, I want to shed light on the simplicity of the gospel and the way Christ modeled us to lead His Church.

Why read *The Abiding Church*? To put it simply, I hope this book will be a "great awakening" to the simplicity of Christ's methodology for leading His Church.

This book is written for Church leaders in all areas of ministry. *The Abiding Church* offers a fresh examination of the process and patterns that Jesus Christ used in His own ministry to create healthy churches. Jesus' methods were revolutionary, yet they were so simple that we might trip over their simplicity. I hope that you are encouraged and find fresh passion for your ministry with each page you read.

I meet many Church leaders in my line of work who have answered God's call to enter the ministry. They are passionate, working very hard, for long hours, and yet they are unsatisfied, seeing little or no fruit for their efforts. Many feel more like a cheerleader or a motivational speaker than a Church leader. Too often, these leaders quit before they ever get to see the fruit of their labor.

Sometimes all you need is a fresh perspective on timeless truths to know that what you are doing is making an eternal difference. This book offers that hope and reminds you that you can follow the blueprint God has for your life, with both joy and fruit, as you are awakened to lead as Christ modeled.

I have been asked many times what fruit people typically see when they take this journey to become an abiding Church. While there are many fruits that come from a church that will walk in obedience to Christ's methods, the most powerful one is transformed lives. People can argue against religion, but not against transformed hearts.

The second fruit that stands out the most to me is the sense of a renewed commitment to stewardship. Stewardship is a built-in characteristic of people walking in proximity with Christ. When you have an Abiding Church, you don't have to ask people to give of their time, treasure, and talents, because they understand their sacred responsibility and stewardship that comes with relationship with Christ.

## *The Swoosh*

Years ago, in prayer, I had a vision of a day when I would author many books that would help spread the gospel of Christ to the nations. During that vision, I saw what I could only describe as a smeared fingerprint. I immediately knew what it meant. In the environment in which I'd grown up, we took the biblical model of anointing with oil seriously. If you have ever taken some oil on your finger and then applied it to a doorpost, to someone's forehead, or to a sheet of paper, you are familiar with the smeared fingerprint that is left behind. In my vision, I had the understanding that I wanted to anoint each copy of the books, which would leave a smeared look on the covers. I wrote this in my journal and left it there.

Years later, as I began to see the dream of authoring Christ-centered books come to pass, I was reminded of this vision. Although I cannot personally anoint every book, I decided to use what I call a *swoosh* to designate that each book has been prayed over. My prayer is that the words in the books published will be anointed by God, bring life transformation to all who read them, and bring glory to God.

## *Workbook Sections with a Journal Prompt*

At the end of each chapter of this book, there are application-focused workbook sections that will help you delve deeper into the material and develop concrete steps to put the abiding principles to work for your individual and congregational needs. In each workbook section, there will be a journal prompt. In Appendix B, you will find the STAR journaling grid, which is designed to help you discover how to journal in a meaningful way.[2]

We want you to understand that journaling is another form of communication with God and can become a lifestyle. This will happen when you feel connected to God through His Word. This connection happens when you read His Word and apply it to your life in the circumstances you are dealing with.

As we move forward in this book, it is important that you understand that this process requires that you learn to "self-feed" with God's Word. You can get a journal to accompany this book, or you may use whatever works best for you. In using the journal, you will experience a process that will help you become a self-feeder. This process will likely continue for the rest of your life. I understand that most people initially feel a little intimidated with journaling, until they come to see that it is not as hard or as complicated as they feared it would be.

## *About The Abiding Network*

The vision of The Abiding Network, of which I am the founder and directional leader, is to assist leaders in creating environments of discipleship to encourage followers to know Christ and make Him known.

Abiding Network was launched out of Catalyst Church in Bentonville, Arkansas, in 2013. This is a support network for church leaders who are active in ministry to know Christ and make Him known in their area of influence.

Our heart is to network individuals, churches, nonprofits, and other groups to support their Kingdom calling. We offer a system of biblical accountability, encouragement, relationship building, and resource sharing to assist in their health and long-term success.

As a network, we have partnered with dozens of churches in many diverse areas. Our website (http://www.abidingnetwork.com) offers some of the organizations and ministries with which we have partnered for Kingdom fruit. As our network grows, we add ministries to our platform so that the network expands as God leads.

The intent of Abiding Network members should be to unite in the common vision to know Christ and make Him known. We want a unity of the Spirit that celebrates what God is doing in our world today.

## Coaching

Many leaders in the business and church worlds need an outside voice for encouragement, accountability, leadership development, and organizational strategy. One aspect of The Abiding Network is to serve leaders in such a capacity—for instance, in seasons of building, transition, growth, relationship development, tragedy, and celebration. Some of the most fruitful seasons of our lives can be birthed out of a mentor or coach helping us process through our journey.

We also are developing many leadership resources that are available to help church leaders navigate the short- and long-term direction and vision of their sphere of influence. I personally have been coached, and I myself coach many leaders in many different ministry and secular environments. I have found coaching to be one of the greatest catalysts to my personal and professional growth and leadership development. Sometimes we simply need a coach, like Paul was to Timothy, to help us grow into all that God intends for us.

## Resources

For more information about The Abiding Network, please visit www.abidingnetwork.com. Media resources can be found at http://www.abidingnetwork.com/Media.

And see my other books, *Abiding at the Feet of Jesus* and *Abiding in Identity*, also published by Sermon To Book.

I appreciate you taking the time to check out these resources in addition to reading this book. Thank you for your interest in The Abiding Network!

## *My Prayer for You*

Ultimately, as an Abiding Church leader, I spend most of my time helping people get to a deeper place with Jesus, a place where they are truly transformed. I have the most satisfying job in the world. I am a Kingdom co-laborer with God and His people. We are all on the same team. My prayer is that you will read the pages ahead with an uncluttered and open heart, that the Holy Spirit will show you how to become the Abiding Church leader He created you to be, and that you experience a new sense of freedom in your ministry.

—*Nate Sweeney*

CHAPTER ONE

# The Hope of the World

The Church is a Whore, but She is my Mother.[3]

The Church is the hope of the world. There is no other group that offers hope like Christ's Church. She is the medium through which He has chosen to reveal Himself. We can gather from Scripture that the Church should be defined by His Presence and carry out His blueprint for humanity.

Despite God's mandate for the Church, we see examples throughout human history of the Church being unfaithful to God and prostituting herself out to false gods, selling out to politicians, and looking the other way when sinful acts were occurring. No matter how defiled the Church became, however, God has always pursued His bride to regain her faithfulness. He has never given up on His Church, and neither should we.

As in Church history, it seems that many churches today have strayed from Christ's model and design for His

Church. This has caused many believers who love God to despise the Church. There has been a mass exodus from the traditional Church, globally, and Church leaders have sounded the alarm for years.

Many today only see a spiritually anemic group of people—identified as the Church—and they are confused, as this group does not line up with the biblical blueprint that Jesus gave us.

In our attempts to stay afloat, we have preached a cheap gospel and peddled a soft savior. We have offered grace without repentance and turned the Church into a consumer buffet that offers appetizers instead of the meat of God's Word.

I think many Church leaders have settled for this status quo, hoping merely to still exist a year from now, instead of thriving like the New Testament Church did.

Leading churches has become a job and paycheck instead of a holy calling. Some people have given up on the Church and declared that her best days are behind her, while some other groups have left the traditional Church model and swung the pendulum to different extremes, offering false teachings and universalism, and trying to make the Church into something other than Christ intended. We must remember that, although the Church may be dysfunctional, she is still the bride of Christ.

I sometimes feel like Paul, speaking to Timothy:

*And I thank Christ Jesus, our Lord, who has enabled me, because He counted me faithful, putting me into the ministry, although I was formerly a blasphemer, a persecutor, and an insolent man; but I obtained mercy, because I did it ignorantly in unbelief. And the grace of our Lord was exceedingly abundant, with faith and love, which are in Christ Jesus.*

*—1 Timothy 1:12-14*

None of us is worthy in our own right to be a servant of God. Yet Jesus has chosen us, sanctified us, and called us to lead the most precious thing He has—His Church. Do you realize the significance of that? God has chosen *you* to lead His people and edify His body. That is a huge responsibility.

In leading His Church, we must stay true to the integrity of His methodology. What was the secret to Jesus' success? Remember that we are under the authority of the Chief Shepherd and that He commands us to "obey those who rule over you, and be submissive, for they watch out for your souls, as those who must give account" (Hebrews 13:17a).

That is a sobering thought. One day, I am going to give an account for the stewardship of the people whom God has entrusted me to lead. I think it's worth spending the needed time and energy to ensure that we are doing the right things for God's people. Hearing the words "well done" from God is not a guarantee for Church leaders, nor will this commendation happen by mistake or happenstance.

There is a popular saying that "the road to hell is paved with good intentions." Intentions, without the follow-through of discipline and faithfulness, will never produce any fruit.

James 1:22 reminds us not to be deceived by merely

listening to the word without being an active participant in what God reveals to us: "But be doers of the word, and not hearers only, deceiving yourselves." I want to be a leader who produces eternal fruit in the vineyards that God entrusted to me. I want to lead like Jesus led.

People are looking to you for vision and direction. Many are willing and ready to follow in sincere loyalty, if you will just lead them. Great leaders arise out of times of turmoil and disaster by doing the right thing.

The twenty-first-century Church is in disarray and confused about her identity, but God is asking you to sound the alarm and send out the wakeup call. The latest research I could find on the American Church is sobering, at the very least.

In America:

- Each year, 3,500–4,000 churches close their doors.[4]

- Churches lose an estimated 2,765,000 people each year to nominalism and secularism. That comes to 7,575 people a day leaving the Church.[5]

- Only 15 percent of churches in the United States are growing, and just 2.2 percent of those are growing due to conversions.[6]

- Each month, 1,400 pastors leave the ministry due to moral failure, spiritual burnout, or contention in their churches.[7]

With numbers like this, some would concede that the

American Church is failing and may even be past the point of resuscitation. And if pastors in these churches and denominations don't make some changes, then I don't have a problem with their doors closing.

But what do we do with these alarming facts? I want to help pastors and churches find health and vibrancy through Christ's model for leading His Church. It is time to arise as the true remnant and become who we were created to be. It is time to say that it's okay to weed out the bad from the good. I believe, as do thousands of pastors around the world, that Christ is still the world's greatest hope and that He chose His church as a conduit. We have to pay attention to the alarms and make the changes necessary to get our churches back to reflecting Jesus.

I pray that, as you're reading here, something inside of you is stirred and you are challenged and encouraged to turn the pages ahead. Every great leader in the Bible had a moment of calling and empowerment when their life paradigm was shifted from a temporal focus to eternal realities. I am hearing of many Church leaders across the globe who are picking up on this message and getting back to the blueprints of Christ's Church. The Church is winning, globally, and people are coming to know Jesus in ever-increasing numbers.

Have you ever stopped what you're doing to ask Jesus how to lead His Church, how to have an abiding Church?

WORKBOOK

# Chapter One Questions

**Question:** Do you see the Church as victorious or defeated, the hope of the world or having already lost to the world? What has contributed to your opinion? How can you gain (or keep) a biblical perspective on the Church?

_____

_____

_____

_____

_____

_____

_____

_____

_____

_____

_____

**Question:** What are potential warning signs that your ministry has become just a job to you? How can a leader who has lost his love for the Church and the passion of his calling find these things again?

_____

_____

_____

_____

_____

_____

_____

_____

_____

_____

_____

**Action:** Read Appendix B to learn about the STAR journaling process.

**Journal Entry**: For your first STAR journal entry, read and meditate on 1 Timothy 1:12–14. Write it out in a personalized form, reviewing your own conversion and call to ministry. Note three areas of decline in the Church that most burden your heart, and then recommit yourself to God's call on your life.

# *Chapter One Notes*

_____

_____

_____

_____

_____

_____

_____

_____

_____

_____

_____

_____

_____

_____

_____

_____

_____

_____

_____

_____

_____

CHAPTER TWO

# What Is a Disciple?

*And Jesus came and spoke to them, saying, "All authority has been given to Me in heaven and on earth. Go therefore and make disciples of all the nations, baptizing them in the name of the Father and of the Son and of the Holy Spirit, teaching them to observe all things that I have commanded you; and lo, I am with you always, even to the end of the age"*
**—Matthew 28:18–20**

If I ask the question, "What is a dog?" we would all have similar answers. Even if we described different breeds or various characteristics, we would all agree on the attributes common to all dogs. However, if I ask ten different pastors to define a "disciple," I am certain that I would get ten different answers.

What is a disciple? A true abiding Church will produce fully devoted followers of Christ; that is to say—disciples. Let's be clear on what a disciple is and what it is not.

Many people receive all their theological instruction

from books or from various instructors who, in some cases, have never opened a Bible. Some folks would say that disciples are produced through a program or process that their local church has put in place. They are told that if they go through the classes offered, at the end there will be a certificate that says that they are a disciple. Other churches simply offer up the generic thought that any person who professes faith in Christ is a disciple. Which is correct?

I think we need to ask ourselves, sincerely: What is a true, biblical disciple? What was Jesus' example of a disciple? What was in the DNA of a first-century disciple? If we don't teach this on the front end, then we do people an injustice. If we don't have a clear understanding of what a disciple of Christ actually is, then how can we fulfill the Great Commission found in Matthew 28:18–20? If we don't know what we're moving toward, then we have no clear measure of whether or not we are being true to our Master's command.

A disciple can be defined as a learner, a pupil, an imitator, a follower, and a reproducer. In Jesus' ministry, I notice a pattern that looked something like this:

- A call to come and see
- A call to a greater commitment
- A call to die to self

Matthew 4:19 says, "Then, [Jesus] said to them, 'Follow Me, and I will make you fishers of men.'" Jesus used this pattern in the initial call of the disciples, as well as in the remainder of His earthly ministry to introduce the gospel.

## *Coaching New Christians*

Like most Church leaders, I am daily inundated with mail, e-mail, social networking, and blogs with new ministry and program ideas that will "revolutionize my church." Many of these are great and, I believe, God-inspired for the person or ministry to whom God gave it.

Many of these programs offer promises of making disciples. They are well put together and are written with passion and ministry in mind. The problem, I find, is that most of these articles and books present ways to make a disciple before ever addressing the heart of the pupil.

These books give the believer steps and processes that can be accomplished on a fleshly plain. They seem to get the cart before the horse. They seem to focus on external conformation rather than anything internal. The ground must be prepared before sowing can be effective. Programs do not make disciples. I know that statement might shock most people in ministry, and that is one of my greatest concerns for the Church.

One of the areas where Jesus was the most dynamic was in His ability to grab a person at the core of his or her being. Christ looked past the outward mask that people presented and convicted their hearts.

When Christ gets ahold of you at the deepest level, you have a decision to make: to follow Him or to reject Him. Getting a new Christian to adhere, outwardly, to a book of principles is not going to produce fruit, nor will it make a disciple. Kingdom fruit is produced by leading people to abide in Christ.

> *Woe to you, scribes and Pharisees, hypocrites! For you travel land and sea to win one proselyte, and when he is won, you make him twice as much a son of hell as yourselves.*
>
> *—Matthew 23:15*

The verse above is chilling. Jesus accused the religious leaders of His day of creating a follower who looked like them but was not pleasing to God. This pupil was worse off than the scribes and Pharisees themselves. Much like the teacher, this pupil worked within a system that looked religious and godly on the outside.

This duplication happens in a lot of seminaries and Christian colleges in America. People go there in hopes of becoming a minister of the gospel and they come out less like Christ than when they began. They, in turn, take this methodology into their churches and the cycle continues.

Christ does not want converts; He wants disciples. To *convert*, by definition, is to change so as to serve a different function.

If you can be converted to Christianity, then you can be converted to something else. Conversion does not produce long-term fruit in the life of a person. Only *transformation* does.

Many converts are educated into a system of religion. They know what the Word says, but it stops there. Belief in Christ or the knowledge of the Bible alone is not enough to be a disciple of Christ.

*You believe that there is one God. You do well. Even the*
*demons believe--and tremble*

—*James 2:19*

I have read of university-trained historians who know more Bible facts than the average Christ-follower yet live as atheists. They put biblical knowledge on the same level as all other historical knowledge. The Scriptures are just another book of writings to them.

The verse above shows that belief alone is not enough to have eternal life. Education never produces a disciple. Education can produce a convert who buys in to the system that is taught. This convert can be trained or educated toward something else later. If this person was never transformed at a heart level, then he simply conformed to some new way of thinking.

Discipleship comes out of an intimate, abiding relationship with Christ. No other way. I think that education is important, but many times we educate our minds at the expense of our hearts. When it comes to God, this is backward. A renewed mind is part of the sanctification process that comes after transformation. The heart must be addressed first.

It is time the Church learns how to move converts to Christians, sinners to saints, and believers to disciples. We must exchange our long-distance relationships with God for close, loving relationships that have daily contact with Jesus. It's more than words on a page; discipleship is about discovery. A disciple allows God to author his faith and through abiding in Christ gives Him permission to be the finisher of his faith (Hebrews 12:2).

The first act of a believer who desires discipleship is permission. You must give Christ permission to be your Lord and submit your will to Him. Many believers in Christ are not disciples. We have fed our humanistic tendencies to give these people "step programs" to accomplish what we think is good.

Self-help books in the Church sell like hotcakes, because people are looking for answers to the problems that they thought would be fixed when they found Christ. Most Christians love a good five-step program or a ten-step self-help book. It helps them to feel that they are in charge when they align their behavior with a certain system. The problem with this is that this is not the personal and utter abandonment that Christ asks of His true disciples.

When we are done, most of the time, we end up either self-righteously proud of our accomplishments or unrighteously condemned for our failures. A disciple is not in control. He has relinquished his control to Christ when he says, "I will follow You."

Programs do not make disciples. I want to be clear that I believe programs do have a part to play in the local church. Programs can help a believer grow, mature, and learn. However, they don't guarantee that they produce healthy, growing disciples.

I knew a pastor who had a congregation of about one hundred people. He was a loving pastor who was faithful to his church. One day, I went to his church website and saw dozens of programs that they were currently offering. How in the world did a church of one hundred sustain that many programs? The answer is: They don't.

His mind-set seemed to be that the more programs he offered, the more chances he had of growing the church. But the exact opposite was happening. His church was not growing at all. In fact, it had become little more than a revolving door that never allowed anyone to stay for long. My heart breaks for him, because he was discouraged and began talking of leaving the ministry.

## *Relationships, Not Formulas*

Jesus' model was all about proximity to Him. God is a very fluid God, and He has an organic nature about Him. As it pertains to His methods, He is not rigid at all. His Word is forever settled in heaven and it never changes, but God manifests Himself in many ways.

The moment you think you have His methods figured out is the moment He will throw a huge twist in your plans. In Jesus' ministry, He did many miracles, but He rarely did them the same way. You could not follow His teachings and say that, "If you want to heal blind eyes, I have the formula from Him to make that happen" (Mark 8; John 9; Luke 19). He is not a formulated deity whom you can figure out.

God fed Elijah over a period in his life in many ways. The ravens came and fed him (1 Kings 17:4–6). An angel came and fed him (1 Kings 19:1–7). A widow was asked of God to feed him (1 Kings 17:8–10). There was no set pattern.

Many of us think we have figured Him out, and we

speak in absolutes as to our findings. Sometimes we preach our experiences as gospel truth and lead others to that same formula. This confuses a lot of Church people and causes many believers to try to imitate your formula, and they end up discouraged. I think it's arrogant and foolish to speak like we have God all figured out.

The abiding Church gives people the secret to living in God's will for the rest of their lives. First, we draw near to Jesus on a regular basis, which allows us to know what He wants to happen in our lives. Next, we follow Him in loving obedience and see His glory proclaimed on the earth. I have to tell you that it's never a formula but fellowship that gives you what you need each moment.

This reminds me of the phrase in the Lord's Prayer, "Give us this day our daily bread" (Matthew 6:11). God gave the Israelites in the desert daily manna (Exodus 16). If they tried to save some for a rainy day, then it would spoil. Trusting that God will provide each day requires faith, which pleases God. God wants us to come to Him, daily, for our sustenance and feeding.

The abiding Church teaches the daily bread model. Doesn't it sound easier to push people to proximity than trying to have a human answer to God questions?

## *The Trouble with Man-Made Models*

I think that man-made corporate models have crept into Church leadership to complement the gospel. Unfortunately, they often end up diluting it instead. We try to run our churches with a corporate business model.

While this can make converts or draw in new members, it isn't enough to create disciples.

Every pastor should understand that there is a business side of the Church that helps maintain fiscal and administrative integrity. The business side exists to allow a legal and thriving environment for ministry to occur. The business serves the ministry, not the other way around.

So often throughout the gospels, we see Jesus doing things that would never be recommended in a modern business class. Often Jesus called people to "come and see" (John 1:39). He called them to discipleship. Jesus understood that for fruit to remain, He had to teach them how to abide in Him (John 15:5).

If you remember, Jesus did not choose hundreds of people to continue His legacy. At the end of three years, He only had eleven men whom He felt were worthy of the term *disciple*. This ragtag bunch of men was the catalyst that turned this world upside down with the gospel message.

Don't trip over the simplicity of this model. If this was Christ's secret to success, then why are we not walking this same method out in our churches today?

An abiding Church learns how to simplify. If your church has to define and clarify who you are and what you're about in more than a few simple steps, then I would question whether the focus of the Church is actually on Christ.

If every person in your church, from the lead pastor to the toddler in the children's ministry, cannot define your church's focus, then it's too complicated.

If your staff is not speaking the same thing as your attendees, then it's too confusing. Christ did not complicate the gospel.

If you notice, Paul's pattern of ministry was to go to a place and then preach the gospel. He did not change things up every week in order to to attract more people. His message was simple and clear.

In the epistles, we see him address Church topics and answer many questions asked of him by the churches. However, his main message, everywhere he went, was the gospel: get close to Christ and allow Him to transform you through repentance. This simplicity produced power as people connected to it and allowed it to change their lives. He used a similar message everywhere he went.

One of the successes that we are experiencing at Catalyst Church, and in our networks, is that we don't use a lot of programs. Everything from the top down is permeated with the DNA of *Knowing Christ and Making Him Known*. We accomplish this through our ministry process: Experience, Grow, Share.

There are many programs that will fit our vision, but we don't try to make them happen. We have ministries that function under the vision and within the process that are designed to point people back to proximity and abiding in Christ.

We want every person in our Church to become a disciple. We understand the programs do not create or make a disciple of Christ, so we limit them. A program can help a disciple grow or help a pupil learn. The only way a disciple can be created is by maintaining close proximity to Christ and intimately abiding in Him.

Our ministries are geared to point people back to Christ and allow them to have an experience in Him, to grow in Him, and then the fruit will be to share Him.

Making disciples is not about adding more programs, or even ministries, but it's about having a vision and process in place that points people back to abiding in Jesus, every step of the way. I don't think this is rocket science or anything new under the sun. I think it is simply Christ's model. When Christ called His disciples, He said, "Come unto Me, be with Me, and abide in Me" (Matthew 11:28; John 15:5).

We must do the same, if we are to have an abiding Church that produces eternal fruit for our Master. We have learned to keep things simple and trust the process we have in place.

Some Church leaders implement new programs all the time. And then, if they don't see immediate fruit, they throw those programs out and try others. I want to encourage you to prayerfully seek God for His plan for you to become an abiding Church, and then stick with it. Don't try to copy another church's model. Get before God and receive what He has specifically planned for you. You can do it. Don't be discouraged, but be encouraged. Remember, simplicity is the best.

# Chapter Two Questions

**Question:** What are the hindrances to making disciples in our churches and culture today? What are some modern opportunities that help in discipleship? Is the Church effectively making disciples of this generation? Why or why not?

_____

_____

_____

_____

_____

_____

_____

_____

_____

**Question:** What is your church's operative mission statement? How does it align with the Great Commission? How well is this mission statement known and understood by your congregation?

_____

_____

_____

_____

_____

_____

_____

_____

_____

_____

_____

**Action:** Keeping in mind the ideas of simplicity, discipleship, and relationship—design a system of evaluation to decide which programs/ministries/structures your church needs to keep, and which are not fulfilling the true purpose of the Church.

**Journal:** Follow the STAR method for Matthew 28:18–20 and its relationship to your church's mission statement.

# Chapter Two Notes

_____

_____

_____

_____

_____

_____

_____

_____

_____

_____

_____

_____

_____

_____

_____

_____

_____

_____

_____

_____

_____

_____

_____

CHAPTER THREE

# Abiding in Christ

*Then, Jesus said to those Jews who believed Him, "If you abide in My word, you are My disciples indeed."*
**—John 8:31**

Discipleship is not about arriving, but about abiding in Christ.[8]

A disciple of Christ has all of the following attributes, which we will explore in the next few chapters:

- Has made Christ Lord of his life and has taken up his cross.

- Has personal abandonment and absolute trust in Jesus.

- Lives in a daily posture of repentance.

- Is in an abiding relationship with Jesus.

- Is a self-feeder.

- Is a reproducer of what he has become in Christ.

How long does this take? I believe, based on Christ's model, that a person becomes a disciple the moment they take up their cross to follow Him (Matthew 16:24). Did you notice that He said "if" in the verse above? "If" is the determining factor as to what will happen next. Most people will not take this step.

Some will take this step the moment they experience God and will begin their discipleship journey. Others will call on Christ for salvation and, years later, will come to the place of taking up their cross to follow Him. In my opinion, a disciple is born when his attitude to Jesus moves from Savior to Lord.

*For, many are called, but few are chosen.*
**—Matthew 22:14**

Many believers have every intention of becoming disciples of Christ. They make lofty plans to make that commitment—at some point in the near future. Like the verse above, we see that many are called and invited to discipleship, but few choose to come.

Like what takes place with the definition of *disciple*, if you ask people what a *Christian* looks like, you will get many different answers. Some people will give you a list of do's and don'ts. If you comply with their list, then you are, in their opinion, a Christian. Others will point to what church organization you are affiliated with. They

will talk about the completion of certain classes or programs as being the DNA makeup of a Christian. Still
others will define a Christian as someone who does
things for God. They are working toward salvation by
outweighing the bad they have done with the good they
are doing.

I challenge you not to fall into any of the definitions
listed here. A biblical Christian is defined as one who is
in an abiding relationship with Christ. To abide means to
continue to remain connected, to make your home with,
or to be in relationship with someone.

What you do for Jesus means nothing unless you are
abiding in Him. Abiding is about fellowship with Christ
and getting to know Him.

## *The Simplicity of Abiding*

*I am the true vine, and My Father is the vinedresser. Every
branch in Me that does not bear fruit He takes away; and
every branch that bears fruit He prunes, that it may bear
more fruit. You are already clean because of the word
which I have spoken to you. Abide in Me, and I in you. As
the branch cannot bear fruit of itself, unless it abides in
the vine, neither can you, unless you abide in Me. I am the
vine, you are the branches. He who abides in Me, and I in
him, bears much fruit; for without Me you can do nothing.*
*—John 15:1–5*

The model that Christ gave us for a follower is so
simple that it confounds the wise of this world. Jesus told
us to simply remain connected to Him. That's it. No ten-
step program or chart of accomplishments. Just stay con-

nected to Him. Abide in Him.

Some key thoughts about John 15:1–17:

- Note the intimacy between Christ and the Father.

- Note the intimacy that Christ wants with us, just like He has with the Father.

- Note the seriousness with which He speaks about bearing fruit and the consequences for those who do not.

- Note the total dependence on Him that we must have.

- Note how our prayer life changes when we abide in Him and have His heart.

- Note how the Father is glorified when we bear Kingdom fruit.

- Note the importance of love in this passage—how walking in His love is connected to our obeying His commands and loving others.

I've met many Christians who hold God at arm's length, afraid to let Him get too close. They attend church, read their Bibles, and pray when something important comes up. Either they have a skewed vision of who God is, which makes them fear Him, or they are sure that God will make uncomfortable demands on their lives.

Jesus does not want us to put Him at the top of our list of "things to do for the day." He does not want us to check off our time with Him like we would check off items on a grocery list or a list of household chores. Jesus wants to be the center of our lives. He wants everything else in our lives to flow through our relationship with Him. This is totally different from just being part of a to-do list.

What does it look like when you are abiding with Christ?

- You spend time really digging into the Bible, reflecting on what is being said and applying it to your life.

- Throughout your day, you assume a posture that allows you to hear what the Holy Spirit is saying.

- You don't look at what people will do for you, but rather you seek out ways to show God's love to others.

- Throughout the day, you find your heart seeking to draw closer to Jesus no matter what is going on around you.

- You see godly fruit happening all around you, not because of your efforts, but because you are in tune with what the Holy Spirit tells you.

If you only viewed your spouse or friend as a

checkmark on your list, the relationship would never last for long. Your relationship with Jesus is no different. Outside of abiding in Christ, you will have an uncultivated soul, overgrown with briars, thistles, and thorns.

The best thing we can do as Church leaders is to push people toward proximity with Christ. This is the definition of a Christ-follower. My ministry in life is to help people get as close to Christ as possible and encourage them to stay there until they have an abiding relationship with Him. I know I am fruitful when they are ready to take their abiding relationship and share it with someone else. There is no greater feeling in the world than seeing people experience Christ in this way.

As you spend time in the Church, and around the Church world, you will notice that there seems to be a tendency to complicate things. Many Christians fall into the trap of thinking that more is better. Many will try to convince you that you need "Christ and..." They will try to add things on top of Christ for your salvation.

Many of these people are goodhearted, but they can lead you astray from abiding. Church leaders are usually the guiltiest in this area. Jesus kept things very simple and spoke practically to people.

So many times, the simplicity of Christ's method is overlooked as being "too easy." People think that there must be more to it than this: "Give me something to do and I'll do it." "Give me a ten-step program that feeds my ego, and I'll be sure and complete it." Do not lose fellowship with Him in your pursuit to know about Him.

The most important thing, moving forward, is that you're abiding in Him. This abiding should never be overlooked in your pursuit to gain knowledge about God. There is a significant difference between the two, and it is easy to fall into this trap.

## *Abide in Christ*

Many of us go out provoked to share about Jesus in a religious way, and we really do more damage than good because we are not connected to the vine. We might be saved, but we are not intimately abiding with Christ, so our lifestyle contradicts the message we are sharing. It is one thing to share with a person that you can relate to their struggles and that you are walking toward holiness. It is walking in obedience and having accountability in your life that helps you on your discipleship journey. That is different from making excuses for an ungodly lifestyle. You are cheapening the gospel and grace when you don't allow your lifestyle to be transformed as you abide in Christ.

> For "whoever calls on the name of the LORD shall be saved." How then shall they call on Him in whom they have not believed? And how shall they believe in Him of whom they have not heard? And how shall they hear without a preacher? And how shall they preach unless they are sent? As it is written: "How beautiful are the feet of those who preach the gospel of peace, who bring glad tidings of good things!"
> **—Romans 10:13–15**

We will have many God-ordained missions, but our sight must remain constantly fixed on making Christ known, no matter what we are called to do. I know business owners who have used their sphere of influence to make Christ known. We have people leading discipleship journey groups at major corporations in Northwest Arkansas. They are using their spheres of influence, using the place that God has put them in, to share the love of Christ. We have stay-at-home moms raising their children in environments that inject Christ into every area of their kids' learning, play, and work.

Think about what you have. First, look at your home, your children, your spouse, and your neighborhood. Begin to ask God specifically for ways to love these particular people. Strategically and intentionally invest in your coworkers, neighbors, family members, and friends. Look for times when the Holy Spirit is leading you to have gospel conversations with others. Know that not every conversation has to be focused on salvation. In fact, until you have established relationships with people, they likely won't be ready to hear what you have to say about God.

Second, partner with what others are doing in both the local church and on a global level. Find a balance of giving time, treasure, and talent to all sorts of mission projects through your local church body.

Go back and read John 15:1–17. Take time to reflect on the heavy, yet simple truth that Christ gives us. What does abiding look like to you? Have you ever looked at your life as dependent on someone else?

Ask God to teach you how to abide in Him. Ask Him to show you areas in your life that need to be cut off and removed, as well as other areas that need to be pruned, so that fruit can grow. Give God permission to discipline and prune that which will make you grow more. If you can walk in this biblical fellowship, then you can introduce this abiding Church concept to your area of influence.

I have a pastor friend who was in ministry for thirty-five years with little fruit to show for it. A few years back, he got hold of this "abiding principle," and he began to teach it to his church. He has been reborn, and his church is thriving. There is life now in their biblical community that is like nothing he has seen in the past three decades. Where he was once looking to retire, he is now re-fired and not slowing down a bit. He is picking up the pace to get this message out to more people.

This can be your church. This book can help you transform your church into the abiding Church that produces fruit that remains.

# Chapter Three Questions

**Question:** In your own words, what does it mean to be a disciple? What does it mean to "abide in Christ"?

_____

_____

_____

_____

_____

_____

_____

_____

_____

_____

**Question:** What is the difference between serving Christ out of begrudging obligation and serving Christ as an overflow of abiding in Him? Which one more accurately describes your ministry?

_____

_____

_____

_____

_____

_____

_____

_____

_____

_____

**Action:** Make a list of what you have—the ministry and mission field that is immediately around you. How can a life of abiding help you reach others more effectively? Now plan specific ways to intentionally build your relationships with those around you to facilitate sharing Christ with them.

**Journal:** Follow the STAR method for John 15:1–17, focusing on your walk with the Lord.

# *Chapter 3 Notes*

# Conformed Versus Transformed

If all the checks and balances were removed from your life, would you be able to regulate your nature and still be a good person?

One of the most powerful things that an intimate abiding relationship with Christ does is to transform us. As Church leaders, I think it is imperative that we understand, clearly, the role that Christ gives us as it pertains to His Church.

We must keep, at the forefront of our passion, the understanding that we are vessels of God. We cannot fix or change anyone else. Let's be honest and admit that we are a work in progress, and, if we had the courage, we would take our masks off and reveal that we don't know what we are doing half the time.

Who are we to stand up and claim to be the answer to our members' problems? That is asking a lot from mere men. If we had the guts, we would preface each sermon with the words, "I am a hypocrite, standing in front of a bunch of hypocrites, telling you to be less hypocritical."

As Church leaders, we sometimes carry the burden that we are supposed to motivate people to do more for Jesus. We get good at getting others to do what we want in our churches. I joke with our church that I took a whole semester in seminary on how to manipulate people and fleece the flock. It always gets a good laugh. But, in all seriousness, so many times we try to get people to do outward things like conform to our church rules and regulations.

And then we wonder why we feel more like cheerleaders or coaches than pastors. We are always trying to rally people to get more involved and to do more. I have some good news for you that should help set your mind at ease: You are not God, and you are not supposed to be the answer to people's problems!

Many church leaders fall into the trap of being the savior and the answer man to their congregations and they allow themselves to be put on a pedestal. The psychological term for this is *messiah complex*. This is when a person feels like he or she has to be others' savior regarding their problems. It feels good for a while—until you wake up one day, isolated and alone, because you allowed men to adore you.

We all know that we are human, and the mistakes will come. The higher you allow people to raise you up, the farther the fall will be when you fail. If you allow people to deify you, then, at some point, they will eventually demonize you, because you will fail.

Many Church leaders never recover from simple leadership mistakes because they have allowed people to lift them up. They love the praise and the accolades they receive along the way—until that praise turns to criticism. Remember, an idol is not necessarily a bad thing in and of itself. An idol can be something good that we put into an unhealthy, exalted position.

As Church leaders, it is our sacred responsibility to lead the Church in the integrity of Christ and steer the ship according to the biblical mandate. This chapter is about getting back to the biblical model of Church leadership. Let's look at what Christ gives as the role of Church leadership.

> *And He, Himself, gave some to be apostles, some prophets, some evangelists, and some pastors and teachers, for the equipping of the saints for the work of ministry, for the edifying of the body of Christ, till we all come to the unity of the faith and of the knowledge of the Son of God, to a perfect man, to the measure of the stature of the fullness of Christ; that we should no longer be children, tossed to and fro and carried about with every wind of doctrine, by the trickery of men, in the cunning craftiness of deceitful plotting, but, speaking the truth, in love, may grow up in all things into Him, who is the head—Christ—from whom the whole body, joined and knit together by what every joint supplies, according to the effective working by which every part does its share, causes growth of the body for the edifying of itself in love.*
> *—Ephesians 4:11–16*

The hardest part of discipleship is walking with people on their journey to brokenness. Discipleship is messy, costly, and time-consuming. Everyone travels on his or her journey at his or her own pace. Learning to walk with people on this journey with grace, truth, accountability, and patience is a work of the Holy Spirit and very difficult on the soul.

The greatest joy of discipleship with people, however, is walking with them on their transformation journey of intimacy with Christ. This is what makes all the investment so rewarding. When people finally get it, and they walk in their God-given blueprint, it reminds you that this is why you do what you do. *Life transformation is the greatest measure of leading people in discipleship.*

## *Church Leadership and Discipleship*

As a Church leader, it is important to understand the parameters of your position. Some responsibilities of a Church leader are:

- Connect the Head to the Body.

- Help people get into proximity with Christ and eventually an intimate, abiding relationship with Him.

- Equip the saints to do the work of the ministry.

- Make disciples by helping develop members spiritually and release them into their area of gifting and influence. This will include reproduction and mentoring spiritual fathers and mothers.

We are called to equip the saints so that the Church can be unified. If we do our part, under Christ, His

Church can grow and mature, allowing each joint and member to do its own part in the Body (Ephesians 4:16). We are not called to do all the work ourselves. We must lead people as close to Christ as we can and then allow Him to do the work of transformation. Conforming people to a set of bylaws, membership commitments, or other church mission statements only works if there is a motivating factor in our lives.

Otherwise, as soon as the outward encouragement stops, people will revert back to the way they have always done things. Worse yet, many such church members only hang around and participate in your church because it makes them feel good, eases their guilt, or feeds their faulty belief that they have to earn their salvation.

They do good to be right with God instead of the "good" being the fruit of right standing with God through salvation. And we wonder why they never seem to grow and remain carnal, unchanged people.

I once met a lady who led the Sunday school program at a large church for many years, until she got offended and left. When I talked with her about why she no longer was a part of that church, she said that she never bought in to the "Christian thing" and only taught Sunday school because she loved kids, and it made her feel good. How sad that she never experienced transformation in Christ but only conformed to the religious organization to fill a need in her life.

## The Danger of Conformation

All biblical transformation begins with nearness to Christ. This is the Christ model. There is no program, class, or sermon series that can transform a person. Getting people close to Christ allows the opportunity for the transformation process to take place and produces disciples.

Many people will choose not to pursue an intimate abiding relationship with Christ. They will simply conform outwardly without any inward transformation. A great example of this was one of Jesus' disciples, named Judas. He was one of the closest to Christ while here on the earth, yet Judas missed the entire abiding concept. Just because you are around Christ does not ensure transformation. However, transformation can only happen in proximity with Christ.

When I say *conform*, I mean to act in accordance or harmony with something; to comply; to act in accord with the prevailing standards, attitudes, practices, etc., of society or a group; to be or become similar in form.

When you conform to something or someone, it is often outward only. You can conform and never buy in to the vision or practice of the organization. You are looking to get something out of it. When it comes to the Church, we tend to think that if we can get the outside lined up, then the inside will be changed, as well. This is not the biblical way.

Conformation is like dealing with a physical symptom without ever addressing the root cause of the problem. If the root is intact, the symptoms will never, fully, be healed.

Years ago, I was diagnosed with psoriasis. The symptoms of this disease are many, but the main one is dry, flaky skin. My body was covered with an inflamed rash that was painful and drained the life from me. The dermatologist gave me shots and topical creams to try to heal the symptoms, but I was only getting worse.

The dirty secret about psoriasis is that there is typically a catalyst that ignites the flareups in your body. In my body, it was streptococcus. What the dermatologist was unaware of was that I had a tooth that was infected with streptococcus, and this was causing the psoriasis symptoms to persist.

Once I got the tooth fixed and the infection cleared up, the other symptoms went away quickly. When I addressed only the outside issue, they never went away. When I addressed the inside—the root issue—the outside change reflected what had happened inside.

The same is true about sin and holiness. Too many times, we tell people to stop doing this or that and focus on changing the outward symptoms while never addressing the inner issue of the sinful heart. This leaves people striving to do better without any real hope of change.

Jesus clearly understood and preached that salvation is an inward work that produces outward manifestations of that change.

Conformation has to have something to be patterned after. What are we conforming to? What are we asking our churches to conform to? That sounds dangerously close to following an idol.

*Little children (believers, dear ones), guard yourselves*
*from idols—[false teachings, moral compromises, and*
*anything that would take God's place in your heart].*
                                    *—1 John 5:21 (AMP)*

God does not want us to have anything between us
and Him. The last place this should be happening is in
the local church, and yet many denominations and
church networks thrive on conforming people to their
own way of doing things.

Many ask for a continual outward conformation and
draw people into systems, not Christ. That sounds dangerously close to getting in the way of God's glory. Billy
Graham once said that he never touched the glory of
God, for he knew the moment he did that God would
remove it from his life and ministry.[9]

All throughout the Bible, we see where leaders chose
the less honorable thing. Many times, they settled for an
idol or an image that produced nothing but problems and
separation from God. They pursued an outside image to
which to conform.

Jeremiah struggled with this when he told the people
of God:

*"Be astonished, O heavens, at this, and be horribly afraid;*
*be very desolate," says the LORD. "For My people have*
*committed two evils: They have forsaken Me, the fountain*
*of living waters, and hewn themselves cisterns-broken cis-*
*terns that can hold no water."*
                                    *—Jeremiah 2:12–13*

The people of God had exchanged the very glory of
God for a form or an image that was lifeless and worth-

less. Second Timothy 3:5 reinforces this thought in that having a form of godliness but denying its power is conformation. People who conform only are not allowing the transforming power of God to change them from the inside out and are aligning instead with religious activity.

*...having a form of godliness but denying its power. And from such people turn away!*
**—2 Timothy 3:5**

It seems to be our natural humanistic tendency to create systems that promote us and our agendas. I think we are drawn to them. But it is a deceptive tool of the enemy to keep people looking at the image or form rather than the real thing. Conforming to anything does not produce internal change. The test is in the fruit that is being produced.

*Two men went up to the temple to pray, one, a Pharisee, and the other, a tax collector. The Pharisee stood and prayed thus, with himself, "God, I thank You that I am not like other men--extortionists, unjust, adulterers, or even as this tax collector. I fast twice a week; I give tithes of all that I possess." And the tax collector, standing afar off, would not so much as raise his eyes to heaven, but beat his breast, saying, "God, be merciful to me, a sinner!" I tell you, this man went down to his house justified, rather than the other; for everyone who exalts himself will be humbled, and he who humbles himself will be exalted.*
**—Luke 18:10-14**

When you address the outside of a person only, it is

an attempt to modify the way they act. Behavior modification works around our sin nature, but it doesn't fix the problem—our hearts.

We try to rearrange the flesh's success to rule our lives and it produces one of two results:

The first result is that of pride. The Pharisee, in the passage above, was quick to condemn all the "other men" (Luke 18:11), especially the tax collector standing outside. He had a list of all the behaviors he did and didn't engage in, which supposedly affirmed his righteousness. He fasted and tithed. He was a faithful attendee of the synagogue. He had to feel pretty good about himself; after all, his definition of spirituality was wrapped up in his actions. He fell in line with everyone else's expectations. Matters of the heart were not important. This produced a pride that blinded him to his true needs. He needed a transformation of the heart, like every man does.

The second result that external conforming will produce is condemnation. We see this both from the Pharisee looking down at the tax collector and the tax collector who is ashamed of himself. Failure and discouragement are the fruits of this kind of thinking. Condemnation from the Pharisee said that the tax collector shouldn't be allowed in the temple, and it also meant that the tax collector agreed.

When we decide that we will be saved through our own goodness, we enter a cycle I call "treadmill Christianity." Your salvation is like running on a treadmill. Every day you are depending on your own strength and ability, running but never getting anywhere. You get tired and eventually fall off and bloody yourself up. When you have been eaten alive with self-loathing and condemnation, you get back on the treadmill in the hopes that your works will put you back into God's good graces.

Over and over you fail and become more discouraged, until, one day, you have enough. You give up and, ultimately, quit trying. Many churches are feeding these types of behavior, while people are growing further away from Christ. Conformation never saved anyone and never will.

## *The Freedom of Transformation*

Transform—change in form, appearance, or structure; metamorphose. To change in condition, nature, or character.[10]

*I will give you a new heart and put a new spirit within you; I will take the heart of stone out of your flesh and give you a heart of flesh. I will put My Spirit within you and cause you to walk in My statutes, and you will keep My judgments and do them.*
**—Ezekiel 36:26–27**

Our goal as leaders ought to be to see others transformed from the inside out—a process only God is capable of working in us. Transformation is a change of our nature. One definition is the process of metamorphosis, like when a caterpillar goes through a change inside of a cocoon. During this process, we don't see a caterpillar or a butterfly—we simply see a cocoon.

A lot happens between the time the caterpillar enters the cocoon and when it comes out a beautiful butterfly. Christ desires to do a work in our spirits that will produce change to our minds, wills, and emotions. He desires that we be so connected to Him that people see less of us and more of Him.

We try to address the physical and mental problems in people while Jesus goes straight to the heart, knowing that a change of the heart will produce a change of the other two.

When you are born again, your heart is changed and alive to Christ. You are a new creation. The Holy Spirit does a re-creative work, and, indeed, you are different.

This is an immediate change that is glorious and amazing. You are empowered for godly living, through the Holy Spirit. At the same time, you still have a mind, emotions, and flesh that have been trained to live after the sin nature.

Part of the transformation process that Christ desires to do in you, involves allowing His Spirit to change you from the inside out. This goes against everything you have ever known and experienced, and it is brutal.

What is happening, if you let it, is the death of your sinful nature, the renewal of your mind, and the dominance of your regenerated spirit. That's biblical transformation.

This process of transformation and renewal of the mind will incrementally change us into the image of God until the consummation of salvation at Christ's return. This is expressed so clearly in the following verses:

*Now, the Lord is the Spirit; and where the Spirit of the Lord is, there is liberty. But we all, with unveiled face, be-holding, as in a mirror, the glory of the Lord, are being transformed into the same image from glory to glory, just as by the Spirit of the Lord.*

*—2 Corinthians 3:17–18*

What a powerful expression of transformation. God has given us complete liberty by imparting the Holy Spirit into us. He, then, proceeds to transform us, into His image, from one degree of glory to the next.

In a true abiding relationship with Christ, this trans-formation will continue and reveal more and more of God to us. At the same time, this will produce a change from our old man into Christ's likeness and image.

We must ensure that we are submitting ourselves to be transformed first and foremost, and then as leaders, we should be more focused on pointing others to Christ so that He can transform them, rather than trying to focus on changing their behavior ourselves.

## *Renewing the Mind*

Another explanation in Scripture is found in Romans, chapters 7 and 8. Paul expresses some seemingly double-minded behavior as he experiences the war that is taking place within his own being. He seems confused and out of control.

*For what I am doing, I do not understand. For what I will to do, that I do not practice; but what I hate, that I do. If, then, I do what I will not to do, I agree with the law that it is good. But now, it is no longer I who do it, but sin that dwells in me. For I know that in me (that is, in my flesh)*

*nothing good dwells; for to will is present with me, but
how to perform what is good I do not find. For the good
that I will to do, I do not do; but the evil I will not to do,
that I practice. Now if I do what I will not to do, it is no
longer I who do it, but sin that dwells in me.*
**—Romans 7:15–20**

At the end of chapter 7, Paul concludes that his spirit-self is alive to Christ, while his flesh-self is alive to the sin nature. In verse 25, he says that with his mind he will choose to serve the law of God. This is a crucial point. Here Paul gives us a nugget of truth that is vital to a healthy walk in Christ: the renewal of our minds.

Your mind involves your thoughts and your will. The human will is the most powerful thing God created. With your will, you can choose to serve God or reject Him.

Paul essentially says that the war is ended when he allows his mind to choose to serve the law of God and he puts to death the body of sin.

In chapter 8, he expounds upon this living in the spirit and having his mind renewed. He said that a carnal mind that sides with the fleshly, sinful nature is at war with God and is His direct enemy.

*For the law of the Spirit of life in Christ Jesus has made
me free from the law of sin and death. For what the law
could not do in that it was weak through the flesh, God
**did** by sending His own Son in the likeness of sinful flesh,
on account of sin: He condemned sin in the flesh, that the
righteous requirement of the law might be fulfilled in us
who do not walk according to the flesh but according to*

*the Spirit.*
**—Romans 8:2–4**

This helps explain why we have so many religious people who have simply tried to conform to the system that is in place in the hierarchy of their churches. They subdue their sin nature as much as possible with self-control. Many times, this produces extreme condemnation and eventual hopelessness, as a conformed individual will always lose the battle against their sin nature.

Go ahead and get back on the treadmill. You will never find peace and rest, until you stop conforming and allow Christ to transform you.

> *I beseech you, therefore, brethren, by the mercies of God, that you present your bodies a living sacrifice, holy, acceptable to God, **which is** your reasonable service. And do not be conformed to this world, but be transformed, by the renewing of your mind, that you may prove what **is** that good and acceptable and perfect will of God.*
> **—Romans 12:1–2**

Here, Paul continues this thought of conformation versus transformation. He strongly encourages us to allow our flesh to be crucified as a living sacrifice. That is the only thing you can do with flesh.

He then goes on to affirm the transformation principle. Do not allow your mind to be conformed to this world's system and way of doing things.

First John talks about the spirit of the world and the spirit of antichrist, which is already at work in this world (1 John 2:18–22). This spirit is contrary to Christ and will produce death and not life. So many believers don't understand the significance of protecting their minds from conforming to the world's system. As abiding believers, we must allow our minds to be renewed by the Spirit of God so that we can stay connected to Christ and follow His will.

Remember, we started this chapter talking about our role as Church leaders to lead like Christ, according to His plan. I cannot find fault in the average church attendee for conforming to the rules that Church leaders have been teaching them. After all, they are doing what they were taught.

In your local church, have you created and cultivated an environment of conforming to religious activity at the expense of a discipleship platform that promotes transformation through an intimate abiding relationship with Christ? If you have, now is the time to acknowledge and begin to ask the Holy Spirit to help you make the necessary changes in your own heart so that you can lead your church to become an Abiding Church.

We must draw a line in the sand and vow, before God, to make these changes in our churches. A pastor who pushes people into the proximity of Christ takes the risk of losing their ministry. In my opinion, I think this is the best thing that could happen. If you have your ministry, then you are not doing God's ministry. It is Christ's Church and His bride. If you want to see abounding fruit, then you must do it His way.

Teaching transformation is slow and tough, as it takes time for people to go through this process and start to see the results on the outside. The key is that it is true and lasting fruit that comes because of the inner issue being addressed and made right.

When you have an abiding Church, it takes all the pressure off you. You are freed up to spend your time and energy doing everything possible to get people near Christ and helping them stay there in order to allow Him to transform them.

You never again have to feel like you have to conform them to anything. Christ becomes center, and you become the "under-shepherd" who helps direct the flock under the leadership and guidance of Christ. That is freedom.

Most religions stress us doing something to be in their gods' good graces. They have us pursuing a god, trying to be good enough for him. Christianity is God's story of Him pursuing us. He says: "I understand your sin and failure, and I have provided a way to be in relationship with you."

Unfortunately, many see the Christian Church as another system of do's and don'ts that focuses on what we are against, rather than what we are for. Remember, the Church is the hope of the world and Christ is the answer to our world's sin problem. We must examine our ministries in light of this. As a Church leader, it is vital to the health of your ministry to allow this abiding principle of transformation to permeate its very DNA. You will see fruit like never before that is sustainable and reproducible. And what is more compelling than eternal fruit?

A person who has an intimate, abiding relationship with Jesus has been, and will continue to be, transformed. This person understands his relationship with God and has allowed that to change his heart. He does not pursue a lifestyle of sin, because he has found the greater joy of being transformed into the image of God (Romans 8:19).

This transformation has removed many of the sinful tendencies from his heart and made his heart to honor Christ. He views his struggles with sin as an opportunity to sit with Jesus and allow His power and love to conquer that sin nature.

The more time this one spends with Jesus, the more he reflects His love and heart. That, my friend, is a disciple of Christ.

WORKBOOK

# Chapter Four Questions

**Question:** Recall a time when you fell into the trap of trying to fix your congregation's problems, motivate them to do more, or control their behavior—i.e., you tried to make them conform. What was their response? How did taking on this self-inflicted responsibility affect your true task of making disciples?

_____

_____

_____

_____

_____

_____

_____

_____

_____

**Question:** How do systems and a focus on conforming lead to pride and/or condemnation?

_____

_____

_____

_____

_____

_____

_____

_____

_____

_____

**Action:** List five to ten of the top "conforming" expectations that are prevalent in your church circles. Next to each, contrast this outward conformity with a true transformation that begins with the renewal of the mind. For example, outward conformity might be to avoid sex outside of marriage. Transformation would be to honor one's body as the temple of the Holy Spirit and to realize Christ is the only One who can provide lasting fulfillment.

**Journal:** Follow the STAR method for Romans 12:1–2 and how it relates to conforming versus transforming.

## *Chapter Four Notes*

CHAPTER FIVE

# The Abiding Church

I am going to speak to you as a leader who desires to have an Abiding Church. This is where the tough part of coaching starts.

You may read something in these pages that stings a little. When that happens, I ask you to prayerfully seek God to help you see your situation through His eyes. Ask Him to lead you, so that you can then lead others.

As a leader, you are responsible for how you lead. If you lead in the wrong direction and people follow, you could be in big trouble. If you are a Church leader, then you will be held accountable for the stewardship of fruit, or the lack thereof, that is being produced in your area of influence as it pertains to raising up leaders around you to help fulfill the Great Commission.

I am surprised at how many senior leaders will sit at a round table at a pastors' gathering and complain about not having good leaders in their churches. It seems the body of Christ is experiencing a leadership shortage. But if you don't have good leaders, then work with what you have in order to create them. If you still don't have good leaders a year or two from now, then it bears looking in the mirror at your own leadership.

Don't blame everyone else for your inability to raise up leaders. God has positioned you in this time and place for that very purpose. If you are not equipped or don't understand this process, that is okay. That is why you are reading this book. I don't think most pastors fail in these areas for lack of trying or desire. Many times, they simply need more training and guidance.

*And He Himself gave some to be apostles, some prophets, some evangelists, and some pastors and teachers, 12 for the equipping of the saints for the work of ministry, for the edifying of the body of Christ....*
*—Ephesians 4:11–12*

We saw in Ephesians 4 that church leaders are called to equip the saints to do the work of the ministry. It's not your job to do all of the work. Your specific role within the church will determine your specific responsibility for oversight and influence. Church leaders were never called to accomplish all of the work of ministry but rather to equip the body of Christ to ensure that the work of the ministry gets accomplished. Grasping this nuance of understanding about your calling will help establish a clear path for you in terms of discipleship and becoming an Abiding Church. What is hindering you from raising up leaders to help accomplish the vision and blueprint God has for the ministry you are leading?

Church leaders are ultimately responsible for the local church under the guidance of Christ and the Scriptures. A church's biblical mission and vision, its health and vitality, and its activities and plans are all equally under the governing care of the leadership. This leadership group assumes responsibility for the local church and must, therefore, be faithful in overseeing, shepherding, and ruling. While this leadership body cannot personally meet all of the legitimate spiritual needs of the church, these leaders must see to it that all of the needs are met through the raising up of co-laborers and fellow ministers.

## *Self-Feeding*

*...holding fast the faithful word as he has been taught, that he may be able, by sound doctrine, both to exhort and convict those who contradict.*
**—Titus 1:9**

*Be diligent to present yourself approved to God, a worker who does not need to be ashamed, rightly dividing the word of truth.*
**—2 Timothy 2:15**

Being an Abiding Church begins with weaning your congregation off of you, your programs, and anything that doesn't directly point them to proximity in Christ. It is easy for people to keep coming back week after week, asking what they are to do. It is easy for them to become more dependent on their relationship with you than on Christ. They send other people your way to ask questions about the Bible and their faith. They have no defense for the hope that is within them when they are challenged.

You must be very careful not to feed these tendencies in people. If they become too dependent on you, then you might be put in a place of idolatry to them. You become their go-between to God. This stunts their spiritual development and is not what the Bible tells us should happen. Christ is the only mediator between God and man. You must push people to become self-feeders.

Many people have been taught that religion is a means to God. I have had people come to me on a regular basis, willing to take whatever advice I give them on big decisions in their life. People asking me simply to tell them what to do and they'll do it. That's scary! I am not God. Telling people what to do is not my job.

If I tell them what to do and it works, they look at me as their answer man and God does not get the glory. If I tell them what to do and it does not work, I am now the bad guy and our relationship is strained. Either way it is unhealthy, and yet I see many pastors leading their churches this way. They like the fact that people come to them looking for wisdom. It makes them feel good and feeds their ego. You have to break the mind-set that people need to come to you for their spiritual growth.

Again, part of becoming an Abiding Church is to wean people off of you and your ministry and point them to proximity with Christ. They have to go through the growth process for themselves. You are not to be put in the place of God. If they began their walk with Christ, drawing from you instead of Christ, then it will be extremely difficult to cut the umbilical cord later in their growth.

However, you are called to be there every step of the way, cheering them on and holding their hands. You are called to lead them on their discipleship journey. We will cover a lot of this in chapter 8.

> *I fed you with milk and not with solid food; for until now you were not able to receive it, and even now you are still not able...*
> **—1 Corinthians 3:2**

> *For though by this time you ought to be teachers, you need someone to teach you again the first principles of the oracles of God; and you have come to need milk and not solid food. For everyone who partakes only of milk is unskilled in the word of righteousness, for he is a babe. But solid food belongs to those who are of full age, that is, those who by reason of use have their senses exercised to discern both good and evil.*
> **—Hebrews 5:12–14**

> *...as newborn babes, desire the pure milk of the word, that you may grow thereby...*
> **—1 Peter 2:2**

What does a biblical self-feeder look like? I remember when my firstborn daughter was learning to eat solid food. She would struggle to get the food in her mouth and, most of the time, it ended up in her hair or all on her face. This drove me nuts, so I would feed her myself or put the spoon in her hand and help her aim for her mouth. She was not learning how to self-feed. In some ways, I was stunting her growth.

I thought it was okay because she was getting more food in her mouth than she would have on her own, but she was not learning to feed herself. Eventually, I had to let go and allow her to grow into the next phase of her development. It was time-consuming, messy, and flat-out frustrating. However, it produced in her the ability to self-feed.

Like a physical newborn, a spiritual babe is helpless and dependent on others. They need a lot of attention and cannot do much spiritually for themselves. This requires them to be fed by others in the biblical community. This is how the Bible says we are to help new believers grow and develop (1 Corinthians 3:2).

Some churches start immediately working on the outward man, telling people to line their actions up with the Church's do's and don'ts. People comply and end up dependent on the pastor or church program instead of on Jesus.

Problems arise when these folks are ready to move on to spiritual adolescence, but we haven't prepared them to do so. We like their dependence on us, and so we stunt their growth by not teaching them how to feed themselves.

If we control their feeding, then they are trained and become dependent on us for their sustenance. They keep coming back to help us fulfill our plans and purposes to build our ministry. This looks good on the outside and even has some characteristics of a healthy church, but it is far from it.

## *Healthy Disciples*

A healthy church consists of disciples who live in an intimate, abiding relationship with Christ. Just because people are gathering in large numbers does not mean health is present. There are many biblical examples of this.

> *Hold fast the pattern of sound words which you have heard from me, in faith and love which are in Christ Jesus.*
> **—2 Timothy 1:13**

> *But sanctify the Lord God in your hearts, and always **be** ready to **give** a defense to everyone who asks you a reason for the hope that is in you, with meekness and fear...*
> **—1 Peter 3:15**

The verses above point to the disciple knowing and understanding his relationship with Christ. Everyone should be held accountable to the passages above.

I know very few Christians who could even give one or two biblical passages to affirm the faith that they profess. How can we be so apathetic to something that is so important? If your life has been transformed, then declaring your faith should be at the top of your list of importance.

Church leaders should do everything we can to raise up leaders who know what their abiding relationship with Christ is all about. The knowledge that accompanies the abiding relationship is so important. Again, I think the missing link is the abiding principle. Just defending the faith is empty without the relationship. If people have been simply sold on salvation, then they will not have the inner desire to be like the verses above. They need transformation.

Is the repetition starting to sink in now? Abiding, abiding, abiding. That is the focus of this whole message here. This message is completely opposite of what most Church leaders are leading their churches with.

> *Therefore, we, also, since we are surrounded by so great a cloud of witnesses, let us lay aside every weight, and the sin which so easily ensnares us, and let us run with endurance the race that is set before us, looking unto Jesus, the author and finisher of our faith, who for the joy that was set before Him endured the cross, despising the shame, and has sat down at the right hand of the throne of God.*
> *—Hebrews 12:1-2*

Jesus is supposed to be the initiator and completer of the faith of disciples, not you (Hebrews 12:2 CJB). If you are raising people up to be self-feeders, then this passage will resonate in your heart. When Church leaders understand that the purpose for all Christians is to self-feed with Christ daily, we can assist those in our care as they walk through that journey. It will allow us to become an Abiding Church.

## *Following Christ's Example*

*Then He appointed twelve, that they might be with Him*
*and that He might send them out to preach...*
        *—Mark 3:14*

It seems that many Church leaders have fallen into the trap that more is better and that complicated is more spiritual. We believe that if we offer more doctrine, theology, programs, operating principles, and series, then we will have success. I only see a few operating principles in Jesus' ministries.

First of all, I see the "get close to Me" principle. Jesus called disciples to Himself, drawing them to a deeper place. Jesus' main point in training was simply being with His disciples. Jesus' new covenant revelation to them was that the law was being fulfilled and that abiding with Him was being instituted.

Unfortunately, when He tried to do that with the masses, many left, saying it was hard to understand or had too high of a cost. Jesus offered this principle to the religious leaders of that day, but they rejected Him as a lunatic. Jesus' focus and time was spent on teaching His disciples. Every day, these men spent time learning from Christ through explicit instruction and by observing how He lived.

An Abiding Church leader keeps focused on the main thing: Jesus. It requires the leader to stop running to the pastor whenever he wants to learn something about the Bible. The pastor teaches his congregation how to understand what is written in Scripture and how to pray. When he plans sermons or conducts small groups, the pastor focuses on pointing people to Jesus. He takes their hands and escorts them to the inner chamber, then waits outside while they abide with Christ.

This is a tremendous change in mind-set for some people. Many pastors are used to trying to fix problems and answer all questions. Instead, teaching these same people to go to God with these questions is what's necessary to make a disciple and have an abiding Church.

Is this too simple? For many it is. We teach the purity of the Word of God as the standard and allow the Holy Spirit to take that Word and transform the pupil into Christ's image. It really is a beautiful thing.

Allow Jesus, not you, to be the author and finisher of their faith (Hebrews 12:2). My role as a senior leader, and even as a believer, has changed as I have come to understand these principles. I have gone from trying to rally people to be a part of what we are doing at Catalyst Church, to asking myself, "How can I bring people close to Jesus?"

When our members have gone through that period of initial transformation—through abiding—then we put them into programs and ministries to help them grow. But the abiding must come first. All we're then doing is putting them into an accountability system that helps keep them encouraged and faithful to continue to remain in Christ.

You can put a disciple in a program or a sequential process to help them grow, but a program will not make an abiding disciple. We'll see more about that in

Chapter 6.

The key is: Everything in the disciple's life has got to flow out of Christ being central. It is not healthy to put Jesus at the top of your daily agenda because you will view Him as an item on a checklist that is to be accomplished before moving on to other things. Instead, everything you do throughout your day should flow through your relationship with Christ. Christ should be the center through which everything else should flow.

## *Spirit of Unity, or Unity of the Spirit?*

*...endeavoring to keep the unity of the Spirit in the bond of peace.*
**—Ephesians 4:3**

The passage above has always amazed me. The thing about this passage that is so neat is the part about the unity of the Spirit. This is much different from a spirit of unity. I hear talk in the Church about the spirit of unity. If we're not careful, we can pursue this spirit and miss out on the main thing.

I have found that people like to rally behind a common cause. People like to feel a part of something and they want to feel included. This happens in the Church, as well. We can rally behind a building project, an outreach ministry program, or a social justice campaign, and all be unified with a common goal. On the outside, this seems healthy. But too many times, I see a spirit of unity instead of unity of the Spirit.

Many times, we are following a plan that is not God-inspired and that keeps us from His best. In Genesis 11:1–9, the story of the Tower of Babel is described. A group of people were rallied behind a common goal—building a tower that would reach the heavens—and they were in a spirit of unity. When the dust settled, God was not pleased because it was a man-made unity and not a unity of the Holy Spirit.

Although man-made unity is powerful and can get a lot accomplished, it can also detract from what God desires to do. The Jews, in Jesus' day, had a spirit of unity that they set to crucify Him, but that was not unity of the Spirit (Matthew 27:22–23). Hatred and jealousy is what drove their united efforts.

An Abiding Church operates on the principle that, if we are all connected to Christ in an abiding relationship, then we will walk in the unity of the Spirit. This unity will produce a peace that molds us together for a common purpose to make Christ known.

I am amazed, at times, at how God is leading me in areas of my life that are so unique and special to me. When I begin to share those with others in the context of my biblical community, we soon realize that He is speaking the same thing to all of us. None of us had previously talked about it or put a plan together to pass the information along. We were just abiding in Christ and walking in the unity of the Spirit. I think this is one of the greatest fruits of an Abiding Church.

When the majority of your community members are flowing in the unity of the Spirit, things seem to work so much more smoothly. Unity is like the lubricant that keeps moving parts from friction. Unity will produce a supernatural peace that sustains disagreements and challenges.

It seems that one of the greatest frustrations Jesus had was with the disciples' inability to "get it." He spoke with simplicity and clarity. He was the best teacher and endued with a limitless measure of the Holy Spirit. Even with all of this working for Him, the disciples still took a lengthy process to grow into what He needed them to be.

Becoming an Abiding Church is not easy, and many people will revert to the status quo and easier way of doing things. Simplicity isn't the same as easy. This is where you must humble your heart and ask God to lead you and your church through the transformation to becoming an Abiding Church. If you will do this, God will give you grace and allow fruit that lasts to come out of your labors.

If more Church leaders saw enduring fruit in their churches, I am certain we would not see the mass exodus of people quitting the ministry every year like we do now.[11]

Is this something you long for? Does something in your heart stand up and say, *Yes!* Take some time before continuing to the next chapter and ask God to expose any areas of your life and ministry that need to be refined under the Abiding Church concept that Christ modeled.

Ask for grace and courage to forge ahead in making the changes necessary to be a church that produces fruit for eternity.

# Chapter Five Questions

**Question:** What is the difference between leading a person on their discipleship journey and creating a dependence on yourself? How can you teach those in your fellowship to "self-feed"?

_____

_____

_____

_____

_____

_____

_____

_____

_____

_____

**Question:** Contrast the "spirit of unity" with the "unity of the Spirit." How can you move from the more natural one to the supernatural one?

_____

_____

_____

_____

_____

_____

_____

_____

_____

_____

**Action:** Ask God to show you areas of your life and ministry that need to be refined. Particularly examine whether you have tried to stand in the place of Christ instead of teaching your church how to seek Him.

**Journal:** Follow the STAR method for Hebrews 12:1–2 and consider how you can help others "look unto Jesus."

# *Chapter Five Notes*

CHAPTER SIX

# Making the Necessary Changes to Be an Abiding Church

By this time, I pray you are reading some things that cause you to pause and think. You may or may not be feeling the need to make changes in your current church setup. Maybe there are a few thoughts that are encouraging your faith to continue the way you are going. Others reading this will be ready to make a complete shift to become an Abiding Church.

In construction, there are times when you can remodel and update the current facility without doing much structural damage. Other times, you have to bulldoze the entire thing and start over. Only your leadership team will know what is needed for this transition as you abide in Christ as a church. To become an Abiding Church, you have to be willing to do whatever it takes, including ripping up the current foundation to transition your church to this model.

Many churches will have a very difficult time transi-

tioning to the Abiding Church model because their habits
of depending on the pastor are so ingrained that making
major changes like this will cause the entire structure to
crumble. Your current model may be so far removed
from the Christ model that a simple remodeling plan is
not an option.

The scary thing about institutionalizing a church is
that it will soon become a museum that people come and
visit to talk about the good old days and what God used
to do. These churches have allowed the "one way we do
things" to prevent people from drawing close to Jesus.
While Sunday school and Bible studies can be a great
way to teach people how to study the Bible and improve
their prayer lives, they often become a part of that to-do
list we talked about earlier. Rather than encouraging
people in their intimate relationship with Christ, these
programs convince people that they've checked the Jesus
box for the week and can then go on their way. Transformation isn't happening here, and congregations know
it, even if they can't put a finger on what the problem is.

An Abiding Church sets itself up to be fluid enough to
follow the revelatory leading of God. Does your church
have current life transformation stories, or do you find
yourself only discussing what things used to be like?

My experience in becoming an Abiding Church happened over a couple of the hardest years in ministry I
have ever known. This was a very difficult season, and
we lost many people and resources during the process. I
would do it all over again, though, after seeing the freedom and fruit that is coming from being an Abiding
Church. I literally "grew" the church in half in my first

year of this process. If we were using a lot of modern church measurements, I would have been deemed an utter failure. However, we had a vision to see our church become an Abiding Church, and our measurements were discipleship, intimacy with Christ, and life transformations. We've seen—and we continue to see—enormous growth in all these areas.

## *Hindrances to This Transition*

Transitional seasons can be brutal, but they are temporary and important to take you from one place to another. They are also a necessity if you are going to grow into the ever-unfolding vision that God has for your church. There are many hindrances that can keep you from transitioning to this new way, but you must remember that it is only a season. It won't last forever.

### Fear of Change

During this season of transition, you may feel like you are in a spin cycle that doesn't end. It takes faith and courage to take this leap. Fear can paralyze you into staying put and not walking out the necessary steps.

I want to remind you that, all throughout the Word of God, we see people who were called who were utterly incapable of performing the task at hand. That is the beauty of the call! You get God-sized vision that can only be accomplished through watching God's miraculous provision. He wants you to live in a posture of faith. If it was easy, then the tendency would be to take control, put faith in self-reliance, and leave God on the sideline.

When He manifests Himself in your life and ministry, everyone will know that He did it, and then He will receive all the glory for it. That is the ultimate result, isn't it?

Be encouraged that God is for you and will see you through.

## The Copycat Syndrome

Many Church leaders have no vision of their own. They are simply copycats who read the latest books and go to conferences in order to do what everyone else is doing. You ask them what God is speaking to them, and they will quote a book or send you a video podcast to check out, that tell you what new thing they are trying. There is no fresh revelation of God for their biblical community. This may be the biggest hindrance I see.

If you don't have fellowship with the Chief Shepherd, then how can you lead according to His plan? If you got marching orders ten years ago but never checked back in, how would you know you were still aligned with the correct battle plans? If you are not an abiding leader, you cannot lead an Abiding Church.

I know some pastors who use other ministries resources for everything from vision, sermon series, small groups, and children's curriculum, to video teachings for their discipleship training. I am not against any of these things—in part. Our church has greatly benefited from being able to implement proven resources that God gave another leader. However, if, as a senior leader, you don't have anything of your own, then I would question the call and vision of God for your church.

I think we should always be aware of what others are doing in Christ's body, so we can learn and be encouraged. On the other hand, I think it is sad when we become so dependent on hearing from the latest conference speaker or the newest release from our denominational headquarters, that we are paralyzed without them. Where is the spoken word from God to your direct ministry context?

I heard one pastor share how he found out that another church had hijacked everything that they were doing and were copying it all for their own use. They had "borrowed" this church's sermon series and even stolen the graphics off of their website and used it as their own. They did not have a fresh revelation from God for their local body, and so they copied what someone else had.

Many people think that ministry is a "one-size-fits-all" proposition. They think, *If it worked for someone else, surely it will work for us.* Utilizing other resources can be beneficial, but if it replaces divine revelation for your local church, it will become a hindrance to your being an Abiding Church because, clearly, the very leadership of the said church isn't abiding in Christ to know His plans. When you get outside of an intimate, abiding fellowship with Christ, you rely upon revelation from other sources. You settle for organizational principles instead of organic, Holy Spirit-led life.

## Attendance and Financial Needs

The biggest complaints and prayer requests I hear from pastors are regarding finances. Too many pastors are concerned most with "butts in the seats and bucks in the buckets." They measure their churches' success by money and attendance. This line of thinking will be a huge hindrance to becoming an Abiding Church, because it's not focused on disciples drawing closer to Jesus. These pastors are growing bigger egos, not devoted followers of Christ.

Certainly, counting people matters, because people matter. However, an Abiding Church counts people as an opportunity to move them into discipleship, and not just as consumers. As we have pointed out in this book, true discipleship cannot happen on a massive scale. It is much more intimate and takes a lot of administrative and leadership resources to accomplish. If you have large numbers consuming resources and not moving into discipleship, then this is a false measurement of health.

Just last week I was given a large document written by the president of a major Christian ministry in America. This ministry is experiencing major hemorrhaging in the areas in which they measure health. The entire document focused on how pastors should consider looking beyond Sunday morning attendance and financial giving to measure the health of their church.

As I scoured the document, I realized that this was newer information being presented, which surprised me. Are we so focused on the measurements of attendance and finances that looking beyond such metrics is new information? With all due respect, anyone can find a way to gather crowds. Life transformation, on the other hand, is much more in depth. My prayer is that there is an awakening in this organization to see beyond their current status and begin to move toward life transformation.

Certainly, money management and head counts matter, but we must be careful that this does not drive our decisions. To be an Abiding Church, you must get your leadership less dependent on money. I've seen a lot of pastors who need to meet the budget so badly that they modify their messages to keep their big donors happy. When we are abiding with Christ, we are in tune with where God wants us to be spending our money, as well as trusting in Him to provide.

> *The rich rules over the poor, And the borrower is servant to the lender*
> **—Proverbs 22:7**

I am disappointed at the obscene amount of debt that the average church in America feels comfortable carrying. One of the largest contributors to this is inflated salaries for senior leaders.

In talking with many senior pastors over the years, I am shocked at the large salaries that many of them are given for the work that they actually do. I don't believe we need to keep our preachers poor, but we do need to be fair. Many senior leaders make a very large amount of money, and then the next person down the ladder makes significantly less. This contributes to high turnover in the lower staff because no one can afford to work long-term for what they're being paid. Constant turnover in a church will cost more in the long run.

Most churches that are discovered to have money problems usually are exposed for their mismanagement of funds. Most are not lacking enough resources. They are simply mismanaging the resources they have. Because so many don't have accountable oversight, it becomes easy to abuse the resources of the ministry for personal gain. The best solution for this is to get some financial experts who are familiar with the inner workings of a church to set things in financial order. This will free up ministry money to help pay down debt and focus on the ministry as a whole. Remember also that God rewards faithful stewardship. If you are fleecing the flock financially, then God will not pour out His blessings on your church. He will not bless unjust stewards. In fact, the Scripture tells us that we will be held accountable for such practices.

> *Shepherd the flock of God which is among you, serving as overseers, not by compulsion but willingly, not for dishonest gain but eagerly; nor as being lords over those entrusted to you, but being examples to the flock; and when the Chief Shepherd appears, you will receive the crown of glory that does not fade away.*
> *—1 Peter 5:2–4*

Fiscal responsibility is a huge point of concern in the American Church today. People already have trust issues with Church leadership. We should not give them any more ammo to shoot with.

I have also come to understand that many Church leaders have poor stewardship of their personal finances, as well. My personal life was a financial mess until I made some life-altering changes many years ago that set me free from being a slave to debt. God challenged me in that, if I could not manage my own finances, then why would He trust me with a church's?

It was a lot of work and sacrifice, but He was faithful the whole time. I have put safeguards and accountability in place in our church to ensure that our resources are handled with extreme stewardship before God and man. We have a board that directs our salaries and ministry budgets based on national averages for our church size and location. I don't think you can be too proactive and transparent when it comes to church finances. I never have a problem sharing about the inner workings of our church finances, because we have nothing to hide or be ashamed of.

I know God has placed a mandate on me to get our church completely out of debt, and we are working vigorously to do so. Whatever it takes to remove this hindrance will be worth the toil in the long run in your pursuit to becoming an Abiding Church. Freedom to teach and preach the pure, unadulterated Word of God is priceless.

I have always believed that the resources for the harvest are in the harvest. When you make disciples, they understand the sacred responsibility for the health of your local biblical community. Again, you don't have to beg disciples to steward their money well and give. That comes as a fruit of abiding. If you want God to prosper your church, then you must be about His purpose. An Abiding Church understands the Father's heart for the lost and will make that the priority that drives them. God will honor this and bring forth the resources needed for the souls to be harvested.

## Egocentric Leadership

Getting your church less dependent on you is a must for an Abiding Church. We touched on this in chapter 5, when we addressed self-feeding, but I think it bears repeating here.

Are you building your church around you? Are you creating a kingdom where you are top dog, or are you helping to build Christ's kingdom? Do you talk using phrases like, "my kingdom," "my people," or "my church"? Do you view the church you serve as your personal real estate? Do you benefit from your church more than God does?

I see a lot of senior leaders who run their churches like dictatorships. Some demand that people serve them because they are the man of the hour. This type of leadership is controlling and not biblical. Leaders like this fear losing people if they let go of control. If they start to let go of control, then they are not certain of what is next, and many will never allow this transition to take place in their churches.

Our role, as Church leaders, is to serve Christ by serving His Church. Humility is one of the greatest attributes Christ taught us, and we should have the fruit of this in our leadership. Our leadership should consist of account-ability to leaders within and outside of our local church.

We see the apostle Paul's pattern of establishing elder-led and -directed churches. The only single voice should be that of the Chief Shepherd, Jesus Christ. If you left tomorrow and the whole thing came crashing down, then I would say that your church has egocentric leadership at the helm and needs transformation.

Get out of the way so God can be lifted up. All roads in your church should not lead to you. You are not the Chief Shepherd. Christ is. An Abiding Church produces leaders and then releases them into ministry to undergird the weight of discipleship development. An Abiding Church will have multiple leaders who are each empowered to use their unique gifts to glorify God.

## Lack of Leadership Reproduction

The second biggest complaint and prayer request I hear from senior pastors is regarding a lack of leaders in their church to help them accomplish the vision God has given them.

> And the things that you have heard from me among many witnesses, commit these to faithful men who will be able to teach others also.
> —2 Timothy 2:2

Many great leaders do a fantastic job based on their charisma and leadership capabilities. The problem lies in their inability to reproduce leaders around them. This cripples their ministries and stunts their church's growth.

As I said in a previous chapter, if you don't have leaders in your church, then you must work with what you have. If, a year from now, you don't have any leaders in your church, then you must take responsibility for not raising them up.

Too many pastors are asking God to bring them good leaders. Most good leaders will already be fruitful in a biblical community and not be looking to move. God has given people gifts in your church that need to be cultivated and raised up. Raising people's ability and willingness to lead takes time and energy. It does not happen overnight.

*David therefore departed from there and escaped to the cave of Adullam. So when his brothers and all his father's house heard it, they went down there to him. And everyone who was in distress, everyone who was in debt, and everyone who was discontented gathered to him. So he became captain over them. And there were about four hundred men with him.*
*—1 Samuel 22:1-2*

It is interesting to read the story of David's "mighty men." God did not surround David with the best of the best polished leaders. Instead, God gave him the opportunity to develop and empower some very dysfunctional people. Many of these later became known as mighty men and great leaders. I asked God years ago to surround me with the best of the best. What I have experienced, much like David, is that He sends me people in the midst of process and asks me to disciple them. The process of discipleship and transformation has revealed some of the most amazing leadership I have ever seen. The best of the best is who I link shields with, but it was a long process.

The point is, God rarely will give you leaders who are already fully mature. Leadership development is a huge part of a church leadership's purpose, yet so many have no idea where to begin. The Abiding Church model helps create a discipleship platform that develops great leaders.

Many Church leaders don't know where to begin on leadership duplication because discipleship is a foreign concept to them. In an Abiding Church, discipleship is the foundation to the ministry platform. Discipleship will ensure long-term leadership reproduction from those whom God brings to you. It allows you to take those who might not look like much in the natural and watch them be transformed into all that Christ has for them. Their transformed hearts will produce Kingdom fruits within your local body.

Too many senior leaders are not around long enough to devote the time to make this happen. They are in town long enough to preach on Sunday and collect their paycheck, and then they are off again to conferences and church plants, leaving their church to fend for itself Monday through Saturday. Many other senior leaders are overwhelmed in shepherding and administration because their culture has allowed most people in the church to become dependent on them. Many are at the point of burnout, simply because they do not know how or are not allowed to raise up and empower leaders into areas of ministry that would free them to simply walk in their role.

If you don't invest in the base God has given you, then it will dwindle away. If you are not able to devote the time and energy, or have others you have trained up do that, then you should resign your post and hand over the reins to someone else.

Remember, you are to equip the saints to do the work of the ministry. *Multi-site* is such a buzz word in the Church world right now. I hear many pastors saying how they have plans for multi-site expansions, while some have a current church structure that is barely getting by. Multiple sites should not even be mentioned if you don't have a strong sending base.

There are plenty of large churches out there that are not healthy. More people and more locations doesn't mean healthier. In fact, in many instances, I see the opposite happening. Butts in the seats do not mean that your church is healthy.

> But the end of all things is at hand; therefore be serious and watchful in your prayers. And above all things have fervent love for one another, for "love will cover a multitude of sins." Be hospitable to one another without grumbling. As each one has received a gift, minister it to one another, as good stewards of the manifold grace of God. If anyone speaks, let him speak as the oracles of God. If anyone ministers, let him do it as with the ability which God supplies, that in all things God may be glorified through Jesus Christ, to whom belong the glory and the dominion forever and ever. Amen.
>
> —*1 Peter 4:7–11*

The verse above is my life verse in the arena of leadership. I am to do everything I can to empower the gifts of God in others so that He can be lifted up.

- Great leaders recognize the gifts and callings in others and use their resources to empower those people to ministry.

- Great leaders are willing to share the struggles and successes of leadership.

- Great leaders submit themselves to a team environment of accountability and unfiltered conflict to get the best out of those they lead.

- Great leaders rejoice when those around them surpass them in their calling. There is no jealousy or competition among the greatest of leaders.

- Great leaders learn to delegate authority and not just tasks. Delegation of tasks produces followers and workers who must be managed, while delegation of authority produces leaders.

An Abiding Church has senior leaders who understand that God desires to use all the gifts in the house to create and release laborers for the harvest.

**Hierarchies Gone Wild**

Another hindrance I have seen is denominations and

church networks that go crazy with hierarchy and policies. I am not against either. I think our churches benefit from both. I actually prefer administration and order because my mind processes this way. However, we can over-organize and lose the organic manner in which Christ wants His church to function. I have seen denominational policy and procedures become a hindrance when they usurp the Word of God and the leading of the Spirit.

I know guys who have been chewed up and spit out over and over by their denomination's hierarchy, and yet they stay there because they don't see any other alternative. They are more dependent on the hierarchy than on God. Unfortunately, in some cases, that is the way they were taught. They were trained in an environment that was about working your way up the ministry hierarchy to achieve glorious "senior pastor status" one day.

I know so many ministers who feel called to minister to youth and children but realize that their denomination or network puts less value on those roles. They leave their calling to pursue a senior role for the prestige and financial gain. This leaves them unfulfilled and empty, because they are not where God called them to be.

Organization and planning are a must. Even hierarchy within the Church is biblical, if it is established in God's Word. If the policy of the organization is placed above getting people close to Christ, however, then there is a real problem.

If an individual church wants to make changes that go against the hierarchy in place, then they are labeled as boat rockers and can be reprimanded or disciplined. I think many churches that are led from the top down will never be able to make the transition to become an Abiding Church.

I have learned to turn the traditional hierarchy model on its side. This created a horizontal hierarchy that has people leading from all different places in the organization, from back to front and front to back. When all are vertically focused on intimacy with Christ, the unity of the Spirit propels the organization forward in unison.

## Consumerism

It seems that many church environments have become very consumer-driven and Church leaders have learned to offer what the consumers want. This has often resulted in an unhealthy culture.

The local church should not exist to feed consumerism. Last time I checked, we were called to serve and make disciples by knowing Christ and making Him known. Consumerism needs to be addressed and resisted by every Church leader. The answer? You guessed it, the Abiding Church.

The Church organism can become an organization that is institutionalized. If this is not curbed, quickly, that organism turns into a museum—a monument of what once was. There is not fresh revelation of what God desires. That is why the Abiding Church is so important.

I love John's writings in Revelation, the second and third chapters, where God gives him a message for the seven churches—*His* churches. God was still speaking then and still is today.

What sets you apart? Many churches in my community have the same stage look and sing the same songs. From the outside, looking in, the organizational aspects of most churches look the same. What is it about your church that God wants to differentiate? What attracts people to your front door? Are they led by the Spirit, because God has been present in your midst, or are they attracted to the show?

If you draw people with a show, then you have to always be on the cutting edge of the creative to keep them coming back. If the show up the road is better than yours, then people will leave and flock to that. That is not the hallmark of an Abiding Church.

If you are relying only on your creative attractions to grow your church, then you're missing the entire message of Christ. People will leave entertained but empty, eternally.

I think the Church should be the most creative group on the planet. I think the Church should be on the cutting edge of inventions and media. We have access to the greatest creative being ever—God. An Abiding Church will combine the natural and the spiritual to create a dynamic environment that glorifies the King. It's not either/or, but both.

The Church offering hope in something other than Christ, however, including entertainment, would be a great injustice. Remember, we are an organism, not an organization. I think many churches and believers settle for humanitarian and social justice programs as a way of trying to fix the human race, instead of offering the gospel and the power of the Spirit to transform hearts and lives.

Christ brings total freedom. If people allow Him to transform them on the inside, then the outside lines up. Offering a cup of cold water in and of itself is not biblical. Building houses in the name of helping my fellow man is not the Christ model. It has to involve the fruit of transformation or it simply is an act of self-righteousness that makes us feel good.

God wants to do a unique work through your expression of His Church. What looks ignorant to us, on the outside looking in, may be what God is speaking to you, and obedience to His calling is critical. I learned a long time ago not to question methods if there is Kingdom fruit being produced. Kingdom fruit only comes from Kingdom methods. If God is in it, then who am I to question the method He chooses?

If you will take your leadership through a season of seeking and abiding, then God will speak. Be ready and willing to obey whatever He says. But expect people to question you and even rise up against you. To be in God's vein takes a courage and a boldness that many lack.

Again, this does not come from a personality or an education. This comes from an abiding relationship with Christ. He will give you the resources to do what He asks, including the boldness and courage. This will be the greatest journey you ever could embark on. I am praying that, as you read this, God will empower you to stand up and lead with His ability from your abiding fellowship with Him.

If God is for you, then who can be against you (Romans 8:31)?

## *What Would Jesus Do?*

> *Then Jesus went about all the cities and villages, teaching in their synagogues, preaching the Gospel of the kingdom, and healing every sickness and every disease among the people. But when He saw the multitudes, He was moved with compassion for them, because they were weary and scattered, like sheep having no shepherd. Then He said to His disciples, "The harvest truly is plentiful, but the laborers are few. Therefore pray the Lord of the harvest to send out laborers into His harvest."*
>
> **—Matthew 9:35–38**

Human compassion is not the only answer to our world's problems. Christ was preaching the gospel and meeting the physical needs of people. He took the eternal perspective first and began to talk about raising up laborers for the harvest. Jesus' definition of a laborer was more than a humanitarian aid worker or a social justice member. His definition is a disciple. A pupil, learner, follower, reproducer. He transformed people's hearts and then sent them out as laborers with the power of the gospel.

These people needed an encounter with a living God to redeem them from the greatest sickness, a depraved heart. He saw that the crowds were bigger than the laborers, and His God-inspired compassion moved Him to send out the twelve disciples in Matthew 10.

The eternal focus is the most important. While He did meet their physical needs as well as their spiritual ones, the majority of people who had their horizontal needs met never made the commitment to discipleship. If you study Jesus' ministry, you will see that when He called them to deeper levels of intimacy, they took off.

This is clearly seen in John 6 as one example. Jesus said He would not commit to these people because He knew what was in their hearts. He said that they only followed Him for the signs and wonders and because they had their bellies filled with the miraculous multiplication of the loaves and fishes. He knew that they were really looking for more than that, but when He began to pull them toward a deeper commitment to live a life of intimacy as His disciple, most went away.

To reiterate, simply meeting people's physical needs with human compassion does them an injustice by neglecting the bigger gospel conversation that we are called to lead them in. Many churches are doing either/or. Some fall into the trap of preaching the gospel and neglect the compassion side, while others do endless humanitarian outreaches that make them feel good but don't give people the message of repentance. This simply is a form of godliness without the power to change, leaving bellies full but hearts depraved.

Many organizations have stepped in to meet the physical needs of humanity coupled with the gospel and as a fruit of their transformed hearts. I have heard countless stories of people who found Christ in a soup kitchen or another compassion ministry. They came in an hour of physical need and found eternal freedom that went far beyond a glass of cold water or some soup.

Other organizations offer temporary hopes in food, clothing, and shelter, but don't have the spiritual aspect

of eternal life to give them. The Abiding Church understands that Christ is the answer to all the world's
problems—spirit, soul, and body. They focus on the
eternal, while not leaving the other needs unmet.

In Matthew 25 Jesus compares the heavenly kingdom
to a shepherd separating the sheep from the goats. The
righteous will inherit the Kingdom, not because of the
compassionate works that they have done, but because
their righteousness comes from their transformed hearts,
as evidenced by their compassion for the "least of these"
(Matthew 25:40, 45). In caring for those in need, the
righteous discover that their acts of compassion are the
same as if they were done for Jesus Himself.

One commentary[12] sheds great light on the famous
passages of Christ about ministering to the "least of these" among us. The acts of compassion were not
performed to be made right with God, or to fill a need of
our common man. The Abiding Church does these things
as a fruit of the relationship with Christ. We understand
that, when we serve in His name, we are His ambassa-
dors, and it's as if we are doing these things directly to
Him.

*What does it profit, my brethren, if someone says he has
faith but does not have works? Can faith save him? If a
brother or sister is naked and destitute of daily food, and
one of you says to them, "Depart in peace, be warmed and
filled," but you do not give them the things which are
needed for the body, what does it profit? Thus also faith
by itself, if it does not have works, is dead. But someone
will say, "You have faith, and I have works." Show me
your faith without your works, and I will show you my*

*faith by my works.*

*—James 2:14*

In this passage, James was reminding us that it is not godly to accept or reject people solely based on their social status. He was addressing Church benevolence and the need for helping one another out. He was not setting a model for works-oriented salvation but saying that the fruits of our salvation will include compassion ministries.

James was also speaking of the Church, not the world. Throughout the Bible, we see many times where God tells us to help those in our spiritual community. Our brothers and sisters in Him should be taken care of in any way possible. Widows, orphans, the poor, and the sick are to be cared for in the body of Christ—another benefit of coming into the family of God. So, James was talking here about believers helping other believers. I am not saying we begin and end in the Church, but he was very specific about helping God's people and not endorsing some global social equality message.

In Matthew 25, Jesus was saying the same thing. He said, "And the King will answer and say to them, 'Assuredly, I say to you, in as much as you did it to one of the least of these My brethren, you did it to Me.'" He says, "my brethren." Jesus said to take care of His family in this area.

Again, I am not saying we must be exclusive at all. I have made it clear that part of our evangelism to the world is compassion ministry, but that cannot take the place of our true calling. We are to preach the gospel.

The gospel combats against poverty, spiritually and physically. When God is released in a person's life, in the abiding way, it opens the door for Him to manifest Himself to meet physical needs in our lives.

I know some atheists who are just as willing to help their fellow man as some Christians. They do it because it allows them to get outside their self-centered world and feel good about helping others. This is great but, in and of itself, will begin and end with the task. The believer, who does the same thing but who offers Christ's love as the source, will plant eternal seeds and give people a glimpse of God's love.

## *Hope in What?*

Hope is such a vital part of life. I heard once that depression occurs when a person gets to the point of hopelessness. Hope is what gives people the energy to get out of bed in the morning.

The Bible talks a lot about hope and addresses the difference between a temporary, earthly hope and an eternal hope. It sounds good to want to gather people together to make a change and offer hope for people. My question is: hope in what?

If we feed the hungry or clothe the naked today, but tomorrow their immortal soul rests in eternal separation from God, what good did we do? Actually, we helped deceive them into thinking everything was okay in their life, because they got their mortgage paid or their stomach filled.

It is such a disappointment for the Church not to see

what is happening. We are giving false hope that ends with the meeting of the physical needs. Again, a fruit of an Abiding Church will be compassion ministry that combines meeting the physical need with the spiritual need.

## *Social Justice?*

God is not moved by need; He is moved by faith. Faith in His Word and faith in the gospel will move Him.

*These men who have turned the world upside down have come here, too.*
> —*Acts 17:6* *(CSB)*

The early Church turned the world upside down, not through social activism or global movements, but through the preaching of the gospel.

Some will say my thoughts here are both narrow-minded and politically incorrect. The answer to those critics is that I follow the way of my master, Jesus Christ, who led through love, grace, and compassion—but the foundation of His words was truth.

Jesus was not a social activist or a political genius. His mind was singly focused on what God had commissioned Him to do, and He did not get sidetracked by socially correct movements that fed the soul of man. He did not try to eradicate world hunger or leprosy epidemics. Contrary to what the disciples thought, He was not there to kick the Romans' behinds and establish an earthly Jewish government. Jesus came to establish the eternal, spiritual Kingdom of God. He knew that, if people would abide in Him, their physical and emotional needs would then be met.

Social justice is a hot topic these days, and many churches do not realize the deception that can be wrapped up in this message. Again, I think some churches are looking to be a part of whatever will keep their doors open for another week.

We all look around the world and are saddened by the decline of humanity that we see. We ask questions like, "If God is good, then why does He allow this to happen?" It seems as if this generation has decided that the answer is to take matters into their own hands and bring forth a global justice message and movement that will set things straight.

The Church should combat this message with the Abiding Church mind-set, instead of stamping our approval on a movement that is not biblical. If the Church was functioning as we should be on a global basis, then we would not have many of the social issues we do have—and there would be no need for the social justice movements we are seeing take place today.

God has already given us all things that pertain to life and godliness. The things we need are written in the books of the Bible—"for doctrine, for reproof, for correction, for instruction in righteousness" (2 Timothy 3:16).

Holiness is not legalism or judgment. We should be holy through the power of the Holy Spirit and call others to be the same. Our standard is Christ. That is why this abiding principle is a must for the Church to arise and be who Christ commissioned us to be.

The problems we face are not world hunger or dominating world leaders, but the humanistic beast that is leading to these horrific situations. You see, outside of a redeemed heart, we all have the potential and capability of debauchery and sinful lifestyles. The difference between me and someone who would allow such atrocities to occur is that the evil living inside me has been subdued by a culture of law and order in the society in which I live.

If all of the laws were removed from our lives, each one of us has the potential to become a murderer and liar, because the beginning and end of our focus is us. We are so concerned with self-preservation and self-promotion that we will do anything to achieve that, even if that means abusing our fellow human beings.

If we buy in to the humanistic mind-set that is promoted in our world today, that man is God and we are what this life is all about, then we are all doomed. If I truly am nothing more than primordial slime that was made by chance and evolved into what I am today, then why does it matter what happens in my life or what I do to others?

The standard of justice would be whatever I deem it to be. Where is the standard of morality if we are all dirt and animals that were not created? For me to call what others do immoral would be putting my own standard of morality onto them. The world tells us that there is no God and that truth is relative to each of our situations. Well, I think we are seeing the fruit of this thought process played out in our world today.

God is the One who changes us into His image and likeness. He is the standard. The Abiding Church will keep this message at the forefront. There should be no muddy waters; people should clearly see that our message is hope in Christ. Everything else is a secondary issue or a fruit of the first.

Too many times we become sidetracked and lose focus. Don't let yourself slip. Be the Church leader who keeps Christ as center.

> *For you have the poor with you always, and whenever you wish you may do them good; but Me you do not have always.*
> **—Mark 14:7**

Should we feel guilty living in a land of prosperity? I don't believe so. I think we should feel the weight of stewardship that comes with the abundance that America has. However, if we are not careful, we will wake up one day and find ourselves under the wrath of the justice of God, because we have turned from Him to our own lust. There is still a large remnant of Christ's Church that remains in America, and God will bless any nation that promotes righteousness.

Being blessed is not about indulgence or gaining "more for me." The Abiding Church recognizes that they are blessed to be a blessing. God will get resources to us if He can trust that He can get them through us to others. If we stop the outflow of God's blessing, then He will hold back the inflow. He wants us to be good stewards of the resources He has given to us.

In the verse above, Jesus made a statement that magnifies this point. People were angry with, and were judging, the woman who poured costly perfume on Jesus' feet and washed them. They made comments like, "We could have sold this perfume and given the proceeds to the poor." Jesus rebuked them by reminding them that the poor would always be there—but He would not, at least not in a physical sense.

For whatever reason, poverty is a constant in every society. When Mary poured out the perfume, Jesus was not concerned with the amount of money that was "wasted." He said that she did the honorable thing toward Him.

Remember, Jesus was not hung up on money. God is not in debt and running short on cash; He paves the streets of heaven with gold. This whole message is not about money or poverty. It's about the more necessary conversation. The Abiding Church will keep, at the forefront, the message of the gospel.

I came across these statistics a while back and, if they are correct, they are astonishing.

- In 2015, U.S. consumers spent $7.5 billion on potato chips, an average of roughly $23 for every man, woman, and child, according to a recent report by Packaged Facts, a market research publisher.[13]

- The National Soft Drinks Association reported that Americans spent a total of $65 billion on soda in 2012. This is far more than other nonalcoholic beverages. By comparison, Americans spent a total of $11 billion on bottled water, and roughly the same on coffee. According to *Time* magazine, the average household spends about $850 per year on soda alone.[14]

- According to a study from 2015, Christians hold the largest percentage of total world wealth (55 percent).[15]

- Tithers make up only 10 to 25 percent of a normal congregation.[16]

- Only 5 percent of the U.S. tithes, with 80 percent of Americans only giving 2 percent of their income.[17]

- Christians are only giving at 2.5 percent per capita, while during the Great Depression they gave at a 3.3 percent rate.[18]

The larger point is what would happen if believers were to increase their giving to a minimum of, let's say, 10 percent. There would be an additional $165 billion for churches to use and distribute. The global impact would be phenomenal. Here are just a few things the Church could do with that kind of money:

- $25 billion could relieve global hunger, starvation, and deaths from preventable diseases in five years.
- $12 billion could eliminate illiteracy in five

years.

- $15 billion could solve the world's water and sanitation issues, specifically at places in the world where 1 billion people live on less than $1 per day.
- $1 billion could fully fund all overseas mission work.
- And $100 to $110 billion would still be left over for additional ministry expansion.

If the Church in the United States would look at the power we have at our fingertips, and begin to abide in Christ, we could see the gospel and compassion ministries flourish all over the world. This would open the door for people to see Christ's love in action.

> And they continued steadfastly in the apostles' doctrine and fellowship, in the breaking of bread, and in prayers. Then fear came upon every soul, and many wonders and signs were done through the apostles. Now all who believed were together, and had all things in common, and sold their possessions and goods, and divided them among all, as anyone had need. So continuing daily with one accord in the temple, and breaking bread from house to house, they ate their food with gladness and simplicity of heart, praising God and having favor with all the people. And the Lord added to the Church daily those who were being saved.
>
> —*Acts 2:42–47*

Here is one biblical example of an Abiding Church. They kept the gospel as the central focus of why they existed, but they did not leave off the other responsibili-

114 · NATE SWEENEY

ties that God gave them. The horizontal, social acts were fruits of the gospel being preached and accepted. One of the greatest outpourings of the Holy Spirit in the book of Acts was Church benevolence.

We see many examples like the one above, where the Church ministered to the physical needs of the people, including the poor, widows, missionaries, and orphans. They did not look to the state to help take care of the body of Christ. They were moved by the love of God, through the Holy Spirit, to help those in need. They even helped the Church in Jerusalem when they were experiencing persecution and could not provide for their own physical needs. Many sacrificed what they had to serve their fellow family members in Christ.

Don't become distracted by counterfeits of the Abiding Church. Eternal fruit comes from eternal principles. Following the way of the world may make you feel better about your depravity, but it will not save a soul from death. God has made it clear that His Word has all the wisdom and knowledge we need to live a flourishing, abiding life.

Following business models may make the organizational side of the Church function smoothly, but these should never replace the organic spiritual formation that only an Abiding Church can accomplish.

We are to use practical tools to complement those things into which God is leading us. Much of what is in God's Word is contrary to the world's wisdom and way of doing things. We will be questioned and even put down for following the Master's way, and yet to reap eternal fruit we must be obedient to Him and His methods.

Take some time to examine your own ministry in this area. Use organization to complement the spiritual formation side of the ministry—not to overtake the organic movement of the Spirit of God.

# Chapter Six Questions

**Question:** Which of the hindrances to becoming an Abiding Church (fear of change, copycat syndrome, finances, egocentric leadership, lack of leadership reproduction, hierarchy, consumerism) do you personally find the hardest to overcome? Which hindrance poses the greatest obstacle for others on your church staff? For the congregation at large?

_____

_____

_____

_____

_____

_____

_____

_____

_____

_____

_____


**Question:** How much time and focus do you spend re-searching and following current Church trends versus time in the Word and prayer? How is an abiding pastor necessary for an Abiding Church?

_____

_____

_____

_____

_____

_____

_____

_____

_____

_____

_____

_____


**Action:** Conduct an anonymous survey among your congregation to answer the following open-ended ques-tions: "What drew you to this church?" "Why do you choose to remain here?" Prayerfully review the answers to see if they reflect a spirit of abiding or if they reveal a hindrance to abiding.

**Journal:** Follow the STAR method to journal about the hindrance to becoming an Abiding Church that you find most difficult. List relevant Scriptures from the chapter and your own study.

## *Chapter Six Notes*

CHAPTER SEVEN

# Tearing Down the Walls

It is interesting to hear about the decline of the average denomination in America. It is hard to gauge all the numbers accurately with so many churches starting up each year, while many others are closing their doors. I take all of these numbers with a grain of salt, but I am still concerned about what I am hearing and have experienced.

I think many churches and church organizations have become institutionalized museums of what God originally intended them to be. If these groups have left the organic connection to the vine of Christ, then I am all for them shutting down.

I am also amazed at how parachurch and nondenominational church networks are seemingly exploding with numerical growth. Many of these are showing signs of health in critical areas of ministry.

I want to be clear that I am neither for nor against certain groups, organizations, or denominations. However, there's a tendency among Church leaders to glorify their particular church group above all others, and I think that needs to be addressed here.

The Abiding Church will be about the Kingdom of God and set aside personal preferences for His glory. There is a lot of division that takes place within the Church over things that really don't matter on the scale of eternity.

> *And the glory which You gave Me I have given them, that they may be one just as We are one: I in them, and You in Me; that they may be made perfect in one, and that the world may know that You have sent Me, and have loved them as You have loved Me.*
> —*John 17:22–23*

One of the last recorded prayers of Jesus revolved around us. He was praying for all of His Church. He wanted us to experience the unity that He and the Father had. He understood that His body needed to move forward, together, singly focused on His methodology. He never meant for us to create systems that divide and separate. Jesus wants us to be in unity. Systems, administrations, and organizational principles should unite the body under the head, Christ.

The greatest miracle that I can see in the New Testament, next to salvation, happened in Acts 2:1. No, I am not actually talking about the outpouring of the Holy Spirit. I am talking about this statement: "They were all with one accord in one place." That takes a miracle of God to bring so many people together under the same vision and direction. Hundreds of Christians under one roof, unified in vision and direction. Now, that is miraculous. That is exactly what should be happening in our churches across the world.

We should have a commonality that connects us and helps us look past our differences. Many times, Sunday morning in America is the most segregated time of the week, because our churches have chosen to let their differences divide them. We have intentionally created clubs in which we allow some in and keep others out. That does not sound like the Kingdom of God or God's love.

## *Parachurches*

*Now I plead with you, brethren, by the name of our Lord Jesus Christ, that you all speak the same thing, and that there be no divisions among you, but that you be perfectly joined together in the same mind and in the same judgment.*

**—1 Corinthians 1:10**

Many churches spend resources, time, and program energy to get people into their doors. If people come, they feel like they are doing well. My experience is that many people in today's world will never darken the doors of a church, not even for a funeral or wedding. For whatever reason, they are offended by the Church and look at all churches as an enemy.

That being the case, why are we trying so desperately to get them to come to where we are? Whatever happened to meeting people's needs where *they* are? Jesus was a genius at this.

He traveled to where the needs were. Lost people don't typically realize they are lost, and they are not looking to be found. They don't understand the language that the average Christian in America is speaking toward them. We tell them they need to be saved, and they respond by saying, "Saved from what? My life is great without religion. Why do I want to mess up a good thing?"

According to Malcoml Tatum, parachurch organizations are "religious organizations that are not operated under the auspices of a particular faith tradition. Within the context of the broader Christian Church, a parachurch organization can be the means to allow Christians from different denominations to come together in pursuit of a common objective. Because the organization is not accountable to any one denomination, the parachurch is free to function within the perimeters of its own charter and has only to account to the members of the organization for any actions taken."[19]

I think the success of many parachurch ministries is that they thrive on finding their niche in the body of Christ outside of the local church context. Many parachurch ministries are picking up the slack where the traditional Church has failed. They are out in the trenches reaching people where they are. They are not concerned about getting people to come to them; they go where the fish are. They find a need in the world and meet that need in the context of where people live, work, eat, and hang out. Where many Church leaders call people to bring their gifts into the local Church body, many others are being empowered by the Great Commission to go into their areas of influence in the middle of the chaos of this world.

This baffles many Church leaders. They make statements like, "That group is watering down their message just to accommodate people." While, in some cases, that can be true, in others they are simply following the command of Christ to go.

I don't believe we should have parachurch ministries at all. I think we should have expressions of Christ's kingdom, pursuing the blueprint that He gave to us. This should be in conjunction with other churches in the body. We should not cut off the toe because it does not look and sound like us. If the Church does not learn to work together, then we will dry up on the vine, and Christ said that the Vinedresser will cut off the branch and throw it into the fire (John 15:6).

## *Workplace Ministry*

Part of empowering your church is authenticating its workplace ministry. I think this is one of the greatest fruits of an Abiding Church. I go back to Ephesians 4:11–12: "And He Himself gave some to be apostles, some prophets, some evangelists, and some pastors and teachers, for the equipping of the saints for the work of ministry, for the edifying of the body of Christ...." God called you to equip the saints to do the work of the ministry. I cringe every time I hear pastors talk about the ministry only happening inside the walls of the church.

They believe that "true ministry" goes on behind the four walls of the church, undertaken only by the pastoral staff. Everything else is just "lay ministry."

I'm here to tell you that there is no separation of sacred and secular when it comes to ministry. If more Church leaders would validate people's workplaces as one of their greatest ministry opportunities, I think we would see more Kingdom fruit being produced in our daily ministry at work. Most people will spend 23 to 35 percent of their lives at work.[20] The majority of these people will develop relationships with coworkers.

If you, as an Abiding Church leader, would stress that the workplaces where your congregation spends so many hours are mission fields, then you will be raising up laborers for the harvest.

Don't be insecure about your church members' commitment level. If you will empower them to be abiding ministers, then they will begin to see fruit as they share the love of Christ in their everyday life. This will produce great joy and greater commitment to what God is doing at your particular church. They will come back, rejoicing that they got to have a part of what God is doing in the earth.

At Catalyst Church, we have empowered people to live out their intimate abiding relationship with Christ in their local context. This has been an amazing journey to watch. We have seen people stop serving consistently within our local church because God has called them to lead discipleship platforms in some of the largest corporations in the world in local offices. We have seen stay-at-home moms pull back some of their church activity in order to lead discipleship in their neighborhoods. This would destroy the passion in some leaders, but for an Abiding Church leader, it is exciting to see. We choke in the dust of what God is leading others to do. We are their greatest cheerleaders and investors. We celebrate how God is using them. It is amazing!

Jesus talked about this in Luke 15:7, when He said, "There will be more joy in heaven over one sinner who repents." Jesus was not taking away from the command to assemble the Church together on a regular basis. He was simply saying that our focus should be to reach the unreached, not just create a club where our own members hang out and feel superior.

I don't know about you, but my interaction with unchurched people in the workplace is small. While I would not trade what I do for anything, I do understand that there are hundreds of thousands of people in my own backyard that my church members are rubbing shoulders with daily. Why in the world would I discourage them from being salt and light to them? My role has to be to teach them how to draw near to Jesus so that they can, in turn, show His love to those around them.

As you grow into an Abiding Church, make sure that one of your main cultural fruits is to equip your biblical community to view their daily life as full-time ministry. Empower them to be Christ in their places of work. Show them how their work can be worship to God and the most fruitful time of their week, as they are ministers to those with whom they spend much of their time.

I know so many pastors who are in a constant struggle, because they are caught in the chains of their denominational or network hierarchy. They feel trapped in a system that will not allow them to be who God is calling them to be, but they have too much tenure to do an about-face and start over.

This saddens me, as they are gifted and have God-breathed vision. My prayer is that the walls that divide and enslave us would come tumbling down, that there would be no schism in Christ's body for any reason. I hope that we all become so wrapped up in an abiding relationship with Christ that we don't recognize the things that could potentially divide us.

WORKBOOK

# Chapter Seven Questions

**Question:** Do parachurch ministries ultimately help or hinder the work of the Church? How could abiding believers fulfill the roles currently being filled by parachurch ministries?

_____

_____

_____

_____

_____

_____

_____

_____

_____

_____

**Question:** Would you see members trading service at their home church with service in the community or workplace as a loss or as a victory? Why?

_____

_____

_____

_____

_____

_____

_____

_____

_____

_____

_____

**Action:** Meet with two or three Church members for lunch this week. If possible tour their workplace. Dialogue about ways you can better equip and support them in reaching the mission field of their workplace.

**Journal:** Follow the STAR method for Ephesians 4:11–16 and journal about the idea of equipping the members for ministry.

## *Chapter Seven Notes*

_____

_____

_____

_____

_____

_____

_____

_____

_____

_____

_____

_____

_____

_____

_____

_____

_____

_____

_____

_____

_____

_____

_____

_____

CHAPTER EIGHT

# Passing the Baton: Synergy of the Ages and Spiritual Fathers

*For David, after he had served his own generation by the will of God, fell asleep, was buried with his fathers, and saw corruption....*

*—Acts 13:36*

*I have fought the good fight, I have finished the race, I have kept the faith. Finally, there is laid up for me the crown of righteousness, which the Lord, the righteous Judge, will give to me on that Day, and not to me only but also to all who have loved His appearing.*

*—2 Timothy 4:7–8*

Following God's plan might not result in you achieving your hopes and dreams. This is a recurring theme in the Bible. Having godly joy does not mean that your circumstances will be ideal. It just means you will have the inner strength that flows from nearness to Christ to complete the task at hand.

If you have put your hope in your retirement plan, you may not want to take this journey of becoming an Abiding Church. The blueprint of God for your life will require you to lay down some personal preferences and earthly luxuries to pursue eternal significance. If you are wanting a cozy life free from danger in this world, stay away from Jesus and the Abiding Church concept.

Remember that a true disciple of Christ is abiding in Him and has come to the point of daily crucifying his own pursuits for that of the Master's (Luke 9:23). Every believer's blueprint is different, but they all require you to lay down your will to take on God's. All of life should be focused on pleasing God. Many of us fix our eyes on temporary things, while God always sees the eternal (2 Corinthians 4:18).

*And do not fear those who kill the body but cannot kill the soul. But rather fear Him who is able to destroy both soul and body in hell.*
**—Matthew 10:28**

If you are abiding in Christ daily, then you will set your affections on the things that matter most in His plan. In turn, this focus will inspire you to lead your sphere of influence with the same mind-set.

Consider many of the early Church leaders and how their willingness to abandon all to Christ ended for them. Some exchanged earthly comforts for the sake of the cross. Others gave up the good opinions of their contemporaries. Many of them were martyred.

John the Baptist was a young man who, according to all accounts, walked in complete obedience and surrender to God, and he ended up losing his head (Matthew 14:1–12). The bigger picture is what drove them to adhere to the plan of God. Again, the message is simple, not easy. Being an Abiding Church leader could turn out badly for you, but what is most important? The eighty or so years you have here on earth or the eternal reward for obeying God?

> *If that is the case, our God whom we serve is able to deliver us from the burning fiery furnace, and He will deliver us from your hand, O king. But if not, let it be known to you, O king, that we do not serve your gods, nor will we worship the gold image which you have set up.*
> **—Daniel 3:17–18**

Christ is looking for leaders who will answer the call to personal abandonment. He will test that in you, and if you follow through, He will be sure to make your life count for His kingdom. I want to be able to repeat the words of Paul, in that he completed all that God had for him and went on to his eternal reward.

## *The Cost*

Count the cost of being an Abiding Church leader. Jesus said that the gospel is offensive and a stumbling block to many. People may hate you for preaching the truth. Others will accept the message and be eternally blessed because of your leadership.

As I've grown closer to Jesus, I've found that there are very few earthly things that even catch my attention anymore. Even though they weren't necessarily sinful, they weren't God's best for me. You can do anything, but you cannot do everything. It's easy to plead the excuse that we do not have the time to do what is asked of us. I don't ever let anyone get away with that excuse. If we view your social media, Netflix account, sports intake, and any other earthly things going on in your life, we can clearly see that there are many things that simply are not eternally founded. This is where discipline and self-denial come in.

> *Therefore, we also, since we are surrounded by so great a cloud of witnesses, let us lay aside every weight, and the sin which so easily ensnares us, and let us run with endurance the race that is set before us, looking unto Jesus, the author and finisher of our faith, who for the joy that was set before Him endured the cross, despising the shame, and has sat down at the right hand of the throne of God.*
> **—Hebrews 12:1–2**

Again, many of these things are not sinful, but they can be weights that easily ensnare you. Christ clearly was our greatest example of this. In these verses from the book of Hebrews, we see the call to give up earthly things for an eternal call. If you are going to live in intimacy with Christ and lead an Abiding Church, it will cost you something.

When you lead people in eternal things, you will draw

the attention of the enemy. Be ready to face these demons with courage and strength in Christ. Be willing to set your face like flint and lead with the power and courage of the Spirit. Remember, an abiding disciple tells God that he or she will do whatever He says, no matter the outcome. Pay the price and reap the eternal fruit.

## *Spiritual Fathers and Mothers*

I came to the realization, a few years back, that some of the seasoned men and women of God in my life were nearing the end of their race. In many cases, these are spiritual giants who have had amazing years of fruitful ministry. My heart broke and awakened at the same time, realizing that it's time for many in my generation to step up and understand the weight of ministry that is falling on our shoulders.

I began, prayerfully, to see the dangerous possibility that a vacuum effect could happen if we don't intentionally prepare for this moment. I also felt the fear and insecurity that comes with the realization that those in my generation are not ready to take on the weight of what was being left. I even prayed, "God, I am not next in line. There are others who are my seniors by many decades who should be carrying this burden." I felt like God spoke to my heart and reassured me that there are many who have not stepped up and accepted the mantle of ministry that was available to them. For some reason or another, they chose not to obey the blueprint that God was giving, and so God was moving on to the next willing servant.

I see many young ministers stepping up to use their gifts to fill this vacuum that has been created. One sad note that I began to take notice of is that many of these amazing, seasoned leaders wait until they are in the last leg of their earthly races to begin to mentor the next generation. They want to have a moment in time to pass on what they were doing, instead of using their whole lifetime to pour into others.

Imagine that you've got a dozen empty water bottles standing open in a line. If you take a full water bottle and try to get water into each of the empty ones in under ten seconds, you're not going to pass much on to the other bottles. Now, imagine that you not only have an hour to complete the task, but that you can also refill the bottle when it becomes empty. How different is it to pour slowly from one bottle to the next?

You see, we have to realize that we are always giving something of ourselves up for the generation that is coming behind. Obviously, we can't duplicate the gifts or callings of an individual, but we can certainly allow knowledge and anointing to be taught to newer Christians—this is how they will learn to abide and continue the cycle of leading consecutive generations to Christ.

My generation needs the wisdom and experience of those spiritual leaders who came before us if we are going to continue the posterity for Christ in the earth today.

*You therefore, my son, be strong in the grace that is in Christ Jesus. And the things that you have heard from me among many witnesses, commit these to faithful men who will be able to teach others also.*
*—2 Timothy 2:1–2*

A true leader has no success without successors. There are dozens of biblical examples, including Christ, of leaders pouring their lives into a few and teaching them to do the same. When did we lose sight of this vital life-giving gift called discipleship and replace it with corporate gatherings?

## *Races Are Won or Lost in Moments of Transition*

What does the passing of the baton look like? I have asked that question many times in my circles and, like most things, many people either haven't put much thought into it or have no ideas on how to answer that question.

In my experience, a great leader does not wait until he is resigning his post to start to look for his successors. Great leaders are constantly working to raise up new leaders who know how to abide in Christ. This gives the leader the strategic flexibility to focus on the next phase of the vision that God is giving him. This is discipleship.

Great leaders understand that God did not call them to do all the work. Ephesians 4 reminds us that He called you to equip the saints to do the work of the ministry. This is a foreign concept to many Church leaders. "Let non-pastors do the work of the ministry?" Yes, that is what Christ's plan was. During the New Testament times, there were no professional clergy. All ministry was done by average Joes with other job training.

I would argue the point that the greatest leaders are the ones who have the ability to inspire others to be who

God created them to be and then help them accomplish that blueprint. The greatest leaders empower.

When I was in junior high, the school got a new track coach, and his charisma convinced me to join the track team. Somehow, I completely missed the fact that this entire sport was all about running, which was something I didn't like to do. After I got past the shock that people did this for fun, I grudgingly followed through with my commitment.

This coach was very good at what he did. I was recruited to run the 4x100 race. This relay consisted of four different runners each running a 100-meter portion and then handing the baton to the next guy, who continued the race. It seemed simple enough, though we spent weeks training how to properly pass the baton.

One day, the coach sensed our frustration that we were spending too much time practicing how to pass the baton and not enough on developing our running. He gave us a firm talking-to. His words were so clear, I'll never forget them. He talked about the fact that it didn't matter if we had the fastest runners in the world if we could not make a smooth pass from one runner to the next. "Races are won or lost in that moment of transition."

This has been ringing in my ears for years, as I have contemplated the Church and what it looks like to transition leadership. I want to pose some thoughts that may help us all in the pursuit of making the biggest spiritual footprint that God will allow in our short years on earth.

As you begin your journey to become an Abiding Church, I cannot encourage you strongly enough to both

seek out a wise mentor and to be a wise mentor to someone else. Constantly seek out the wisdom of those who
have already wrestled through these things. Be willing to
pass on what you've learned to someone else. Remember
that age is unrelated. Your mentor might be younger in
years but older in Christ.

> Let no one despise your youth, but be an example to the
> believers in word, in conduct, in love, in spirit, in faith, in
> purity. Till I come, give attention to reading, to exhorta-
> tion, to doctrine. Do not neglect the gift that is in you,
> which was given to you by prophecy with the laying on of
> the hands of the eldership.
> **—1 Timothy 4:12–14**

Many young ministers should take note of those leaders that God has placed in your life to speak into you
specifically. Many of them will not force their experience on you. You have to take the time to serve them and
listen in precept and example.

## *Synergy of the Ages*

At my church, we talk a lot about synergy of the ages.
The word *synergy* can be defined as the interaction of
elements, which, when combined, produce a total effect
that is greater than the sum of the individual elements.
What can we do to merge the four individual generations
alive on the earth today and create a sum greater than
each individual piece? How can we celebrate the past as
a foundation to build on for the future? How can we
honor what others have done before us, but transition

that into reaching the generations to come? How can we pass the baton to the next generation in a way that sets everyone up for success?

*I sent you to reap that for which you have not labored; others have labored, and you have entered into their labors.*

**—John 4:38**

*For when one says, "I am of Paul," and another, "I am of Apollos," are you not carnal. Who then is Paul, and who is Apollos, but ministers through whom you believed, as the Lord gave to each one? I planted, Apollos watered, but God gave the increase. So then neither he who plants is anything, nor he who waters, but God who gives the increase. Now he who plants and he who waters are one, and each one will receive his own reward according to his own labor. For we are God's fellow workers; you are God's field, you are God's building. According to the grace of God which was given to me, as a wise master builder I have laid the foundation, and another builds on it. But let each one take heed how he builds on it. For no other foundation can anyone lay than that which is laid, which is Jesus Christ.*

**—1 Corinthians 3:4–11**

These verses clearly show that none of our ministry should be ours. It all is for the King and His kingdom. We should not strive to have a personal legacy as much as we should strive to invest in God's kingdom. When the Corinthians were fighting over position and who would lead whom, it was labeled as carnal, immature, and divisive.

If I build my kingdom, it dies with me. If I do my part

to build God's, then it will see fruit long after I am gone. For me to pass on the stewardship that God has entrusted to me, I have to give my time, treasure, and talent to the next generation. Kingdom fruit lasts forever.

Sometimes you sow, sometimes you reap, but ultimate Kingdom investment produces the fruit of God giving the increase and receiving the glory. Don't be afraid to let go of the ministries and programs that you're proud of if you find that they aren't drawing people to Christ. If they don't help others abide, they aren't worth the effort, time, and money.

> God does not have any grandchildren; each generation must experience God for themselves.[21]
> **—Tommy Tenney**

I believe the best thing we can leave behind to the spiritual generation coming behind us is the Abiding Church message and a healthy group of disciples who are able to meet with Him regularly and carry on whatever work He has for them.

Proximity to Jesus will give us the tools and resources needed for every situation that may come. Getting people close to Christ will give them the ability to succeed in any arena that God plants them in no matter the time in history or the location. This will also give you the power to thwart and defeat any plan the enemy comes against you with.

Church leader, you are responsible to steward the call of God for you and do whatever you can to pass on the

Abiding Church message so that those who follow will have that experience with Him for themselves. My heart aches to think about a generation that does not know God or the works He has mightily performed in my life. Let us do our part to ensure that the generation after us knows how to abide in Christ.

# Chapter Eight Questions

**Question:** What is the cost of discipleship for you right now? Think of someone you admire from biblical or Church history. What cost did they pay to be a disciple?

_____

_____

_____

_____

_____

_____

_____

_____

_____

_____

_____

**Question:** "Races are won or lost in that moment of transition." How are you preparing now to pass the baton to the leaders who will come after you? Are there areas in which you have been building your own kingdom instead of Christ's?

_____

_____

_____

_____

_____

_____

_____

_____

_____

_____

_____

**Action:** Call or visit someone who has been a spiritual father or mother to you. Discuss transitions and mentorship and ways to prepare the next generations for spiritual leadership.

**Journal:** Follow the START method for 2 Timothy 2:1–2.

## *Chapter Eight Notes*

_____

_____

_____

_____

_____

_____

_____

_____

_____

_____

_____

_____

_____

_____

_____

_____

_____

_____

_____

_____

_____

_____

CHAPTER NINE

# Answer His Call

*...holding fast the word of life, so that I may rejoice in the day of Christ that I have not run in vain or labored in vain.*
**—Philippians 2:16**

*And say to Archippus, "Take heed to the ministry which you have received in the Lord, that you may fulfill it."*
**—Colossians 4:17**

I want to appeal to your eternal purpose side for a moment. A Church leader who is willing to lead an Abiding Church understands the eternal weight that is on his shoulders.

When you look at things in light of a few generations, you can miss the big picture. Jesus most often spoke of eternal things. He told us not to fear those who could kill the body, but to fear the One who has the power to destroy you in hell.

I ask you to consider prayerfully the spiritual footprint

that you've made up until this point. If Jesus called you home tomorrow, would you be satisfied with the kingdom legacy and heritage that you are leaving behind? Will your spiritual footprint die with you or outlive you? Did you fulfill the calling and blueprint that Christ has for you? If not, what are you doing to accomplish that?

These are scary questions that many people don't ask until it's so late in the game that they miss the opportunity to successfully complete their race. The average life expectancy in America is seventy-eight years old.[22] Now, how old are you? How much of your life has passed up until this point?

If you are going to fulfill the mission that you have received from the Lord, then a wakeup call may be needed. This information is not to depress you, but to help you recognize the seriousness of life. We are not promised to live to the average life expectancy. All God asks is that we fulfill our calling. That will be different for each of us.

Don't spend your entire life and ministry running and laboring in vain. Make the necessary adjustments now to be a Church leader who will see God's kingdom advanced through your life and centuries beyond.

*You did not choose Me, but I chose you and appointed you that you should go and bear fruit, and that your fruit should remain....*

*—John 15:16a*

## *Your Job Is Sowing*

Working in the fields is hard work. In my early childhood years, I had the privilege to work on a farm during the summer doing all kinds of tasks. None of those tasks was ever easy. However, it was so satisfying to see the plentiful harvest that would be reaped as a result of this labor. It was long hours of work, work, work. Becoming an Abiding Church leader is very labor-intensive and tiring, but it is the most fulfilling work possible when you see the fruit of your labors.

Many times, we feel pressure to perform for God or do things that will get us in His good graces. I want to look at some biblical thoughts on producing fruit. First of all, we don't call anyone to leadership, God does. We are not responsible for the decisions that people do or don't make. We have the ability and responsibility to test the call and help people discover and grow in it.

Remember that an Abiding Church leader understands that his role is to get people in proximity to Christ. That is the definition of success. If we can get people to healthy, thriving relationships with Christ, then transformation can occur, and the fruit of abiding will be evident. Jesus said in the passage above that He has appointed every one of us to bear fruit that would remain, fruit that would continue to reproduce more and more fruit.

I am of the mind-set that, if I am faithful to that which God has called me to, and if I keep doing that, then the fruit will produce. An Abiding Church leader recognizes that it's God who gives the increase. Paul said, "I planted, Apollos watered, but God gave the increase" (1Corinthians 3:6). I am not responsible for the increase. I am not responsible for the fruit. I am called to sow, water, or whatever God commands. He is the One who does the supernatural increasing and fruit production. He is the Lord of the harvest.

I always loved the verse in Isaiah 55:11: "So shall My word be that goes forth from My mouth; it shall not return to Me void, but it shall accomplish what I please, and it shall prosper in the thing for which I sent it."

God's Word does not fail. I have always understood that if I will put the Word of God first, and make it the central focus, that He will ensure that it is not wasted.

Remember that Christ is the living Word. John 1:14 tells us that the Word was made flesh and dwelt among us. Getting people into proximity to Christ is the same as getting them saturated with the Word of God. That just makes me happy. It takes all the pressure off of me feeling responsible for making something happen. God gave me His Word, and when I obey it and apply it, then it will reproduce.

Let's look at the parable of the sower found in Matthew 13:1–9, 18–23. Jesus talked about the sower, who was sowing the Word into four separate kinds of soil. All of the types of soil received the seed, yet only one of the four yielded any crop.

I'm not going to unpack this entire parable, as there is so much we could explore, but the point I want to make is that the sower did his job. He was faithful to do what he was called to do. People have to have prepared hearts and be an in environment that allows the hindrances to growing to be removed. The Abiding Church concept does all of those things. Are you starting to see the abiding principle throughout scripture yet? Discipleship helps people process the sown Word in their life on a personal level.

Sometimes by failing to focus on what is most important, you will find yourself doing the wrong thing. However, if you will stand up and lead your church to prioritize an abiding relationship with Christ, then everything else will line up and fall into place.

God's Word will not return void (Isaiah 55:11). The soil of your congregants' hearts will be ready to receive the planting of the Word. The hindrances to producing fruit will be removed, and fruit that remains will flourish.

If the farmer plants corn and cultivates it, in a healthy environment, then it will produce corn. An Abiding Church that sows the Word and cultivates people by pushing them to proximity to Christ will produce eternal fruit. These abiding followers of Christ will turn around and express the love of Christ to others with the Father's heart.

## *The Time Is Now*

*Do you not say, "There are still four months and then comes the harvest?" Behold, I say to you, lift up your eyes and look at the fields, for they are already white for harvest! And he who reaps receives wages, and gathers fruit for eternal life, that both he who sows and he who reaps may rejoice together. For in this the saying is true: One sows and another reaps. I sent you to reap that for which you have not labored; others have labored, and you have entered into their labors."*

*—John 4:35–38*

Jesus is looking for laborers in His harvest. Too many leaders have lost sight of the harvest and how we can invest in it. These days, there is no sense of urgency or haste as it pertains to the commission that Christ is speaking about. If we don't change our paradigm, then we will miss the opportunity for harvest.

Farmers understand that you don't get to pick and choose when is the best time for you to go out and reap your crops. Many times, due to weather and other uncontrollable circumstances, there is a very small window of time for you to get the most out of the yield.

Abiding churches understand this, too, and since their members are always striving to be close to Jesus, they understand that the time to act is now. God will supernaturally put you in places that you would not have been if you were not abiding in Him. He will cause you to be a reaper of the harvest, often reaping where you have not sown.

The neatest part in the passage above is verse 36, in my opinion. Jesus makes it clear that he who sows and he who reaps will rejoice together, because they will recognize that together their labor has produced eternal fruit. Fruit that will outlast them. Fruit that will be seen in all of eternity. If that does not get you excited, then I don't know what will.

The Abiding Church will see this take place on a regular basis, and it will energize you and other Church leaders even more to continue on this path.

Finishing strong, endurance, and longevity are all so

important. It really does matter how you live your life. Jesus wants you to be productive in His fields and produce eternal fruit that remains. He wants you to be connected to Him and follow Him at all turns. He wants to abide in you and you in Him. He wants you to accept the call that He has committed to you and see you fulfill that to the end.

## *Run Your Race*

> *For we dare not class ourselves or compare ourselves with those who commend themselves. But they, measuring themselves by themselves, and comparing themselves among themselves, are not wise.*
> **—2 Corinthians 10:12**

Don't compare your ministry with others', but create what God has put in your heart for your church. We become jealous when we compare others' polished product with our own work-in-progress. You don't know what it took them to get to the place where they are. You don't know the hours of sacrifice that it took them. Maybe you're not called to do what they are doing. Maybe on the outside they look successful, but they have no health in their community. There are a million reasons not to compare yourself with others. The best is that God gave you what He gave you and said that you will be judged on how you steward that. If you are faithful in that, then He will give you more.

Hearing the words "well done, good and faithful servant" (Matthew 25:21) is not guaranteed. If God has given you ten people in your sphere of influence, then do whatever it takes to push those ten to an abiding relationship with Him. Faithfulness reaps the reward, every time. I have never known a faithful person whose gifts and calling did not make room for them. I have known very charismatic people and successful businessmen who have created a model church that seemed to be doing well with a lot of people showing up, only to find later that there was no character to maintain the man-made structure.

If you will follow the blueprints that God laid out for you, then you will have a simple, clarified plan of action that will produce eternal success.

## *Does My Work Matter?*

We all deal with those days when we wake up and struggle with the questions, "Does my life matter?" "Am I really making a difference?" "Can I look back over the past years of my life and see where other people's lives are better for having me in them?" These are very real questions that I think should be asked and examined.

Can I be honest with you? If you are not walking with God and fulfilling His eternal purposes, then your work won't matter when it comes to eternity. Having a beautiful church with a fabulous worship band that writes its own music is great. But unless people's hearts are being transformed, they have no lasting value. Being the most popular church in town with the coolest pastor is only valuable if people are growing close to Jesus and making the sorts of changes that will impact the rest of their lives.

This is what makes God's desire to have fellowship with you so great. He looks past everything else in eternity and spends one-on-one time with each of His children. That is the sign of an amazing father.

> For I know the thoughts that I think toward you, says the LORD, thoughts of peace and not of evil, to give you a future and a hope.
> —*Jeremiah 29:11*

God is not a deity devoid of relationship. He has always been intimately involved in human history. The verse above attests to the fact that not only does He have a plan for humanity, but He also has a plan for you and your life specifically.

He gave this verse through Jeremiah to a group of people who were heading into decades of captivity. He flat-out told them, "Even though things look bleak now, and you are being taken as captives, My plans and purpose for your lives are still good and hopeful."

He created you the way you are and He needs you to be that person. I call this God's blueprint. Too many churches believe that the minister is the pastor in the pulpit preaching the message. But the Bible says that we are *all* ministers. You must get this in your soul: *You* are a minister for God, as is each person who is sitting in church beside you. You are to take your gifts and minister as a good steward. As an abiding leader, you must create an environment where this concept is established, celebrated, and allowed to flourish.

A steward is someone who manages the goods or property of someone else. God is going to require you to use the gift He gave you, and He will hold you accountable to how you did. Some of you will read this, and insecurities and fear may try to creep in because you don't feel like you have what it takes to be a minister for God. Well, join the club. Fear, insecurity, and pride are no excuse to avoid being a minister.

God deserves the glory. This happens when you yield your will to Him and, in obedience, minister in the way that He created you to minister. Don't compare yourself with anyone else. You may be called to do something that is challenging and requires a lot of faith. Don't let this throw you! God wants the glory and He will stretch you to do things for Him beyond your capability so that no one else can claim the credit but Him. God uses ordinary people to do extraordinary things, and that way He always gets the glory.

A *blueprint* is defined as a detailed outline or plan of action. Part of your walk with God is the revelation of His blueprint for your life. As you grow in God, you will discover the uniqueness of His design where you are concerned. God created you for a specific purpose and has given you gifts that are special to you.

He needs you to be you. If two of us are identical, then one of us is unnecessary. Even identical twins are each unique in God's eyes!

## *Four Principles of a Godly Blueprint*

### 1. God-Breathed

*...Being confident of this very thing, that He who has begun a good work in you will complete it until the day of*

*Jesus Christ.*

**—Philippians 1:6**

*For of Him and through Him and to Him are all things, to whom be glory forever. Amen.*

**—Romans 11:36**

Your blueprint has got to come directly from God. If you want to have eternal success in life and bring Him glory, you must submit to His blueprint. This is why abiding is so important. Hearing His voice and allowing Him to lead you according to His plans is crucial for lasting fruit.

### 2. God-Empowered

*And let us not grow weary while doing good, for in due season we shall reap if we do not lose heart.*

**—Galatians 6:9**

*But those who wait on the LORD shall renew their strength; they shall mount up with wings like eagles, they shall run and not be weary, they shall walk and not faint.*

**—Isaiah 40:31**

It's easy to start a race or a journey. There are a lot of people at the starting gate. There are a whole lot less at the finish line. If you want to have success in God's kingdom, you have to allow Him to empower you to the finish line.

It is easy to tell God that you've got it from here and that you don't need Him. This will leave you laboring in your own strength and ability. Other times, you will get distracted and off course. Allow God to be the leader and follow His blueprint, closely, so that you don't grow weary and disqualify yourself from the race. Remember that Jesus said that we need the empowering of the Holy Spirit in order to be His witnesses and complete the blueprint.

### 3. God-Fulfilled

*Therefore, we also, since we are surrounded by so great a cloud of witnesses, let us lay aside every weight, and the sin which so easily ensnares us, and let us run with endurance the race that is set before us, looking unto Jesus, the author and finisher of our faith, who for the joy that was set before Him endured the cross, despising the shame, and has sat down at the right hand of the throne of God.*
*—Hebrews 12:1–2*

A disciple allows God to author his faith and, through abiding in Christ, gives Him permission to be the finisher of his faith. If you are going to successfully navigate God's blueprint, you must allow Him to bring the fulfillment. Do you trust that God knows what He is doing and that He can do it better than you? Of course He can. Are you going to allow Him to lead and commit to following Him?

Let God bring the fulfillment of the plan. Again, if it is of God, then it usually will be beyond your scope of completion anyway. He will put you in hopeless situations so that you will rely on Him, and when He delivers you, it will be accompanied by the miraculous. Remember, if you allowed Him to author your blueprint, then why would you try to be the finisher? Let God fulfill it and make it happen.

## 4. God-Glorifying

> ...that in all things God may be glorified through Jesus Christ, to whom belong the glory and the dominion forever and ever. Amen.
> —1 Peter 4:11b

God's blueprint for your life comes down to one thing: bringing Him glory. Your happiness and comfort are not the priority. His blueprint for your life is not about you. God does not do what He does to make you comfortable. The quicker you realize that your life is about bringing Him glory, the quicker you'll stop fighting things that make you uncomfortable. Allow God to be glorified in every part of your daily life. Pointing people to Him will bring you greater joy and peace than you ever imagined.

Kingdoms rise and fall. Nations are here one day and gone the next. God's plan for your life is eternal. Jesus accepted the call, cost, commitment, abandonment, and scorn, and His death mattered. There is dignity, honor, and legacy available for the true disciples of Jesus. We all will die, and, when it happens, you want it to count beyond your physical years on earth.

Momentum will be either forward or backward. You're either growing or regressing. The bar is set high because this is a Kingdom mission. It's all about counting the cost. You will answer that question at the end of your life. Will you do what it takes to abide in Christ and lead others to do the same?

Take some time to prayerfully consider what it is that God has created you for. You may be on a good path to where He wants you to be; if so, you should continue on with His direction. But you may be on the wrong path and need to realign yourself to the blueprint that God has for you.

Ask God to speak to you specifically on this topic. This reflection is the first step in leading an Abiding Church. If you yourself don't have abiding fellowship with Christ, then how can He use you to lead others in this way?

Write out a plan to take some practical steps in accomplishing that which God speaks to your heart about the blueprint for your life. This may take minutes, days, or months, and it will change as you grow in your relationship with Christ. Try to use the four principles given here to ensure that the blueprint is God's. Then do the same as it pertains to the ministry that God has you leading.

# Chapter Nine Questions

**Question:** How would you describe your spiritual footprint up to this point in your life? Would you say you have been fulfilling God's blueprint or your own?

_____

_____

_____

_____

_____

_____

_____

_____

_____

_____

_____

**Question:** What are areas in which you have been faithful to sow, but where you have not yet seen the harvest? Are there instances when you have reaped from another's ministry where you did not sow?

_____

_____

_____

_____

_____

_____

_____

_____

_____

_____

_____

**Action:** As described at the end of the chapter, pray about and write out a "life blueprint" and a "ministry blueprint." Make sure you are guided by the principles of making it God-breathed, God-empowered, God-fulfilled, and God-glorifying.

**Journal:** Follow the STAR method for John 4:35–38.

## *Chapter Nine Notes*

_____

_____

_____

_____

_____

_____

_____

_____

_____

_____

_____

_____

_____

_____

_____

_____

_____

_____

_____

_____

_____

_____

_____

CHAPTER TEN

# Never Underestimate the Power of the Gospel

The chief danger of the 20th century will be religion without the Holy Ghost, Christianity without Christ, forgiveness without repentance, salvation without regeneration, politics without God, and heaven without Hell.[23]
**—William Booth, founder of the Salvation Army**

*I charge you therefore before God and the Lord Jesus Christ, who will judge the living and the dead at His appearing and His kingdom: preach the word! Be ready in season and out of season. Convince, rebuke, exhort, with all longsuffering and teaching. For the time will come when they will not endure sound doctrine, but according to their own desires, because they have itching ears, they will heap up for themselves teachers; and they will turn their ears away from the truth, and be turned aside to fables. But you be watchful in all things, endure afflictions, do the work of an evangelist, fulfill your ministry.*
***—2 Timothy 4:1–5***

I hear much talk about how the human race is inherently good overall, and that the Church should awaken that goodness inside of people. That is not biblical. This New Age thought has confused a lot of Church people and has taken away from the Abiding Church message.

We are all born into a sinful nature that separates us from God and His holiness. We are all self-centered and need to recognize our depravity. That is why the Church has to keep the gospel message at the forefront of our mission.

The gospel shows us our sin and our need for a savior, as well as introduces us to the Savior. The proclaimed truth of God's Word gives people the revelation they need to decide to obey God or reject Him. Without the message of the proclaimed gospel, people are left to their own ideas and interpretations as to what makes them acceptable in God's sight.

The gospel is good news. It is very confrontational, and it will expose each individual's weaknesses and sin, but then it immediately gives us hope in Christ.

The gospel is the power of God. It offers a life transformation from the kingdom of darkness into the kingdom of light. It gives people the ability and authority to renounce Satan as their father and call upon God, to be adopted into His family.

*For I am not ashamed of the Gospel of Christ, for it is the power of God to salvation for everyone who believes, for the Jew first and also for the Greek. For in it the righteousness of God is revealed from faith to faith; as it is written, "The just shall live by faith." For the wrath of God is revealed from heaven against all ungodliness and un-*

*righteousness of men, who suppress the truth in unright-*
*eousness....*
**—Romans 1:16–18**

*He who believes in Him is not condemned; but he who*
*does not believe is condemned already, because he has*
*not believed in the name of the only begotten Son of God.*
**—John 3:18**

*For "whoever calls on the name of the LORD shall be*
*saved." How then shall they call on Him in whom they*
*have not believed? And how shall they believe in Him of*
*whom they have not heard? And how shall they hear*
*without a preacher? And how shall they preach unless*
*they are sent?*
**—Romans 10:13–15a**

What should break our hearts is the fact that those who are outside of Christ are already condemned. They already have judgment pronounced against them. We sit around and argue about the same topics we have for many centuries, while all the while people pass us by who are under the wrath of God.

We have the hope and good news to release them from that, but we choose to focus on other things. We need a great awakening to this fact. What breaks the Father's heart should break ours, and what He is passionate about, so should we be.

We cannot afford to miss this vital role of the Church. The Abiding Church realizes the vast stewardship of the gospel message proclaimed. Do not underestimate the power of the gospel. So many churches are looking for the holy grail of ministry to cause their church to grow.

The gospel is offensive. But that is not a reason to stay silent! When we preach the gospel with love, we are sowing the seeds as God has commanded us to do. The condition of the soil where it lands is not in our hands.

The message is so simple that we miss it, over and over. Jesus commands that we proclaim His message of the gospel. In it is the abiding principle. People are hungry for the truth and want real answers to their real-life issues, even if it means hearing the painful truth that comes in the confrontation of their sin through the gospel.

> ...that if you confess with your mouth the Lord Jesus and believe in your heart that God has raised Him from the dead, you will be saved. For with the heart one believes unto righteousness, and with the mouth confession is made unto salvation. For the Scripture says, "Whoever believes on Him will not be put to shame." For there is no distinction between Jew and Greek, for the same Lord over all is rich to all who call upon Him. For "whoever calls on the name of the LORD shall be saved." How then shall they call on Him in whom they have not believed? And how shall they believe in Him of whom they have not heard? And how shall they hear without a preacher? And how shall they preach unless they are sent? As it is written: "How beautiful are the feet of those who preach the Gospel of peace, who bring glad tidings of good things!"
> **—Romans 10:9–15**

There is so much power in the proclaimed Word of God. These verses from Romans talk about the gospel being the power of God unto salvation. There is no greater power on earth than a soul being saved from eternal separation from God and the bondage of sin.

If we are bold enough to preach the truth, then it will give people the opportunity to have faith in the truth, which opens the door wide for God to demonstrate the truth. We come to salvation by faith. This is a foundational verse that many use to share the love of Christ.

The rest of the passage goes on to talk about how salvation is dependent on whether or not someone has heard the gospel. Hearing depends on someone speaking, and speaking is in direct relation to being sent. The Abiding Church realizes this fact and creates an environment of empowered laborers who are going out and proclaiming the Good News.

## *We Are All Called*

*And He said to them, "Go into all the world and preach the Gospel to every creature. He who believes and is baptized will be saved; but he who does not believe will be condemned."*

*—Mark 16:15–16*

The Abiding Church puts the burden of the gospel and the Great Commission on every one of us, not just the leaders (Matthew 28:18–20). Jesus told us all to go. He did not send out a few Church leaders or call the pastors to be the only ones to go. That is not the case. We are all missionaries. We are all called to be on the mission with our Savior's message.

I have heard every excuse in the book as to why churches don't do this, but what it all boils down to is disobedience. Are you going to obey the command to go? Are you, as a Church leader, going to lead your church into the front lines of where the harvest is? Or will you go into compound mode and expect the world to come knocking at your front door?

We are called to take the gospel to the world while not bringing the worldly system into our house. It's that simple. If we are estranged from sinners and speak in languages they don't understand, then how are we to expect that they will hear the proclaimed Word? Or when they hear it, do they only hear hypocrisy and criticism because we speak without the relationship to back up the confrontation?

The God of the Bible is a sender by nature. He is a missionary God who has sent His people into the world since Abraham. In the Old Testament, He sent prophets like Isaiah, Daniel, Jeremiah, and Jonah over cultural boundaries. He sent His Son, Jesus Christ, to earth to live as a man, in a particular time and place, with a particular people, as a missionary in a sinful culture. The Father also sends the Holy Spirit to Christians, so that we, like Jesus, might also live as missionaries in our culture.

A search of the Scriptures will unfold a passionate God who pursues His people. He desires that all men come to salvation and He was willing to give His best, His Son, Jesus Christ, in our place as a sacrifice to make that happen. Understanding His heart will help you to pursue steps to follow after that.

We should be on the mission every day of our lives to bring the gospel to our world. You need to get comfortable expressing this thought to the people you lead. We are all missionaries. This will take biblical teaching and training. You will need to take the time to properly lead people into this line of thinking. Some will get it right away and start on the mission, while others may take years to develop the necessary hunger to take the gospel to their sphere of influence.

The key is that, as an Abiding Church leader, you express the heart of God properly to your church on a regular basis. At my church, I interweave the "knowing Christ and making Him known" message into the fiber of every one of my sermons. Most times when I meet with leaders, I remind them why we exist with talk of vision and encouraging life-transformation steps. We encourage our church to be a catalyst in our world to help others know Christ and make Him known every time we get together.

This is not just a vision statement to us. This is the entire foundation upon which Catalyst Church NWA is built. There is no mistake what we are about, and people know that from the moment they encounter our church.

As the leader, you must set the tone to line up with what God says in His Word and never stray from that. We are all missionaries and should act accordingly while holding each other responsible for that stewardship.

## *Teaching Our Children to Abide*

Don't remove yourself so far that you can't be salt and light to the people around you (Matthew 5:13–16). Instead of sheltering our children from the culture, we need to openly discuss, from a biblical worldview, what is going on in the world.

I remember, a few years back, when my seven-year-old was watching a movie, and she asked me to sit with her, and so I did.

Throughout the movie there were some things that I didn't like, but they were not really horrible, so I just let it go. Then, toward the end, there was a blatant attack on Christianity, and I got pretty frustrated.

I grabbed the remote to turn it off, when I felt the Holy Spirit remind me of my fatherly duty to disciple her in the nurture and admonition of the Lord. So, instead of turning it off, I paused the show and took the next ten minutes to put what we just saw into the context of a biblical worldview.

She asked a lot of questions, and we answered them together based on what the Bible said. It was an amazing teaching moment for me. Since that time, I look for every opportunity to bring biblical context to my children, wherever we are and whatever we are doing.

It was so refreshing to me when, months later, we were at a friend's house and I overheard her telling one of her friends about our conversation. She shared with clarity the discussion we had. It was so amazing that she was able to remember all of what we'd talked about. I saw, firsthand, the power I had to disciple the next generation with the Word of God. Instead of her parroting the admonition that "we don't watch things like that," she was able to intellectually bring the biblical worldview into the discussion. That is so much more fruitful.

I have had Christian parents come to me who are

struggling with the lifestyle their college-aged student is living. They talk about how they raised them in a Christian home and sheltered them from all the worldly things that they are now doing. Some have asked for me to help convince their kid to live out what they believe. The answer I give back is that it seems they are.

Children rarely buy in to the "because I said so" answer that many Christian parents give. They tell their kids to do it "because the Bible says so" and never gave them any teaching on why God says this is the best way to do things.

The kids get to college and realize there is a big world out there, with many other worldviews that contradict the Bible, and so they go exploring. The convictions of their parents are not theirs because the children did not experience the truth themselves. They were just told "because."

I am not making blanket statements here or questioning anyone's parenting skills. All I am saying is that we owe it to our kids to view our culture through the biblical worldview. If we shelter our kids, then all we are doing is caging the sinful nature instead of allowing God to transform it.

Here are a few things that have helped me in leading my own kids as well as other disciples in my sphere of influence:

- **Learn to be relevant without compromise.** Don't be afraid of culture. Watching and listening to culturally popular, age-appropriate movies and music with your child, and talking about the things that are in conflict with the Bible is a great start. This doesn't have to be a lengthy conversation every time, either. Once your child is proficient at it, simply starting a discussion by asking, "What in that movie did you think was not biblical?" is enough.

- **Engage people with the Great Commission while not being sucked into a sinful lifestyle.** A system of accountability in your church helps to combat this. If you're trying to build a friendship with an unchurched person from work, meeting them in their comfort zone typically bears more fruit then a simple invite to your church. Learn to enter into their context with truth, not compromise. The apostle Paul mentioned becoming as all to possibly win one. (1 Corinthians 9:22)

- **Bring theological context when you engage culture instead of running from it.** Culture brings a variety of ideas. Some are in line with the Bible, some are opposed, and some can be redeemed. Assuming that everything that is not strictly "Christian" is automatically evil is damaging. Assuming everything that is labeled "Christian" is ok for consumption is wrong as well. We do our children a greater service if we teach them how to recognize what the Bible says rather than shielding them from everything. You might love a popular book series and want to share them with your middle schooler. Be careful to talk about what the Bible says about the content. Help them see what truth is and how these books are different from real life. This gives them the tools to engage and not run from culture.

- **We need to understand the world in which we live.** Then we can begin the transforming work of the gospel in our culture by contextualizing the good news of Jesus. A biblical worldview is not something you hear discussed much in today's Church. Our worldviews have been founded in many other things like, nationalism, politics, media, and pop culture. So many times, we don't recognize the difference. In Acts 17 Paul was able to engage the culture in Athens because he had understanding of it. He clearly brought the gospel conversation through his understanding of their culture. If you struggle with something, of course you should stay away from it. You need to do some research about things that people around you are talking about and prayerfully consider whether or not they are things you can handle.

- **Abide in Christ.** When you abide in Christ, you learn to process culture through this lens. Your life is a daily mission for your King. This will ensure that you are led to the place of ministry that He has for you on a daily basis. This also combats against falling away into deception or a sinful lifestyle because you engage the culture with Christ's leading. He does not send you out there alone or power-less.

There are more thoughts we could expound upon, but I think you get the point. We are not called to draw back from our culture but to invade it in love.

Remember, the early Church's example. We see these guys going to some of the most godless places on earth to share the gospel message. Paul used his Roman citizenship to get into spheres of influence that the average Jew could not. He, also was able to understand his culture enough, in Acts 17, to address them in language they could understand.

## *Loving Sinners*

The Word tells us that love covers a multitude of sins. Jesus never excused people's sin, but He also never lambasted them for it either. He loved them and gave them grace. Remember that the definition of love, from John 1:14, is grace and truth—as that is how it describes Jesus.

Pure love finds a balance of both. Love brings truth to the surface and gives grace to cover sin. Pure love offers grace all day long but holds people accountable to the truth of God's Word. I think this is one of the best defini-tions of love I've ever seen. It brings a great biblical balance to the conversation.

If you're going to catch fish, you have to go where they are. Jesus did a great job pointing the disciples to where the fish were. He gave us a great example of a person being in His culture, maintaining godly integrity, and sharing the gospel all the while. He used His influence in these pagan contexts to inject the gospel and point them to repentance.

He was so much in the midst of sinners that He was accused of being a sinner, a drunk, possessed, and a blasphemer. He was vilified for being a friend of sinners, and yet He never stopped.

## *Therefore, Be Bold*

It seems, many times, that the art of sharing our faith has become lost. Many churches do not emphasize this, and so many Christ-followers are not making Him known. Others have overcomplicated this simple command that Christ gave us.

> *...praying always with all prayer and supplication in the Spirit, being watchful to this end with all perseverance and supplication for all the saints—and for me, that utterance may be given to me, that I may open my mouth boldly to make known the mystery of the Gospel, for which I am an ambassador in chains; that in it I may speak boldly, as I ought to speak.*
> *—Ephesians 6:18–20*

> *Him we preach, warning every man and teaching every man in all wisdom, that we may present every man perfect in Christ Jesus. 29 To this end I also labor, striving*

*according to His working which works in me mightily.*
**—Colossians 1:28-29**

Paul asked for prayer in the verse above so that he would have the boldness to fulfill the Great Commission in bringing the gospel to his area of influence. Please take this message seriously and do whatever it takes to make your Church an abiding one. You will see eternal fruit if you are willing to do so.

I heard an interview recently from Penn Jillette, a famous Vegas performer and self-professed atheist. His thoughts were very interesting to me. He said that he does not have a problem with Christians sharing their faith because, if he was a Christian and understood the significance of heaven and hell like they did, then he would tell everyone he came in contact with about the message of Christ: "Same as if I saw a person in the street about to be hit by a bus. I would not stand by and watch as they unknowingly got hit. I would yell and scream, until they heard me and got out of danger." He went on to say that he respects Christians for standing up for their truth and wondered why more professing Christians did not seem more urgent to share about Christ, if they truly believed He was the only way to God.[24]

It is interesting to me that a nonbeliever can make this point so clear for me. If you sincerely believe that the preached gospel is the only way for people to find eternal life, then why in the world aren't we doing more to get that message out?

If we as Christians, and Church leaders, would take this same approach and understand the great power in the proclaimed Word of God, we would see our churches transformed. That is the power of an Abiding Church. It will understand this and do everything possible to alert people to the gospel message and point them to proximity with Christ.

When you get people into an intimate abiding relationship with Christ through discipleship, you don't have to compel them to make Christ known. Disciples recognize the sacred responsibility and will walk this out as those who are abiding in Christ. Again, if we simply get this abiding concept into practice, everything else will fall into place.

The buck stops with us as leaders. Christian consumers will kill the Abiding Church movement if we cater to them. Don't allow your church to become a consumer buffet. Do not allow anything to stop you from preaching the gospel. Don't you ever underestimate the power of the gospel preached.

# Chapter Ten Questions

**Question:** Would those who know you say that the gospel is central to your life? Is the gospel central to your church? What is one way you can give the gospel greater prominence in both your life and your church?

_____

_____

_____

_____

_____

_____

_____

_____

_____

_____

**Question:** How can a parent find a balance between overprotecting and overexposing their child? How does teaching your children to abide in Christ help resolve the tension between these two extremes?

_____

_____

_____

_____

_____

_____

_____

_____

_____

_____

**Action:** "Love brings truth to the surface and gives grace to cover sin." Ask your spouse, kids, coworkers, and/or close friends if you are falling short in either truth or grace in your relationships. Listen prayerfully to their responses and evaluate whether or not you have an attitude that could be hindering the power of the gospel in your life.

**Journal:** Follow the STAR method for 2 Timothy 4:1–5 and journal about the centrality of the gospel.

# *Chapter Ten Notes*

CHAPTER ELEVEN

# Empowered to Be an Abiding Church Leader

*I will stand my watch and set myself on the rampart, and watch to see what He will say to me, and what I will answer when I am corrected. Then the LORD answered me and said: "Write the vision and make it plain on tablets, that he may run who reads it. For the vision is yet for an appointed time; but at the end it will speak, and it will not lie. Though it tarries, wait for it; because it will surely come, it will not tarry. Behold the proud, his soul is not upright in him; but the just shall live by his faith."*
**—Habakkuk 2:1–4**

I have always loved this passage of scripture, as it gives a good example of an abiding leader who is leading God's way. Habakkuk's posture in verse 1 is that of seeking, humility, and meekness. He understands that it is God's voice that must be heard in order for him to be an abiding leader.

If you are an Abiding Church leader, you will lead like this. You have to get the plan from God, and then make it plain so that others can follow in your leadership. If you are abiding in Christ, then you will follow after God's vision. If you are following His vision, then He will bring the provision to make it happen. Let go of the burden and release it to God. It's His purpose and His fulfillment for His glory. Don't worry or wonder how it all will happen or come to pass. Simple obedience in an abiding relationship will be successful, every time.

Verse 4 reminds us that the proud man is not upright, but the one who walks in faith is. Remember that becoming and leading others into an Abiding Church is going to push your limits and require personal abandonment and absolute trust and faith in Him. That is why abiding is so vital. You won't maintain that posture of faith if you are not close to Jesus on a daily basis. You will grow weary and bow out if you try to do this in your own strength. Abide in Him.

Verses 2 and 3 talk about how it may take a while to accomplish God's plans, but that they will come to pass. We should be planning regularly and numbering our days to get the most out of them. We should have strategies and chronological orders to leading our churches with vision, into the future.

On the other hand, we should look for moments and seasons when God comes in and messes up our plans. God can use your planning; however, be careful not to get so focused on your plan that you miss God's desiring to come in and bless you with a special moment.

We should be like Habakkuk, who set his face to listen when the Lord was speaking. This can only happen in an abiding relationship with Christ. Unfortunately,

Habakkuk did not get to witness the fruit of his prophetic calls back to God. The people continued to be distant from what God was doing. However, this again proves the point that Habakkuk's ministry was not about him or his legacy. Traditional leadership would label his leadership a failure. When you are abiding in Christ, you do your part and trust God with the fruits. You simply obey and trust that God will get glory from your life.

## The Person of the Holy Spirit

From Genesis to Revelation, the Holy Spirit was an active participant and, yet, many Christians have no clue about Him. His credentials as God are seen in passages like:

*Then God said, "Let Us make man in Our image...."*
*—Genesis 1:26a*

*In the beginning God created the heavens and the earth. The earth was without form, and void; and darkness was on the face of the deep. And the Spirit of God was hovering over the face of the waters.*
*—Genesis 1:1–2*

*When all the people were baptized, it came to pass that Jesus also was baptized; and while He prayed, the heaven was opened. And the Holy Spirit descended in bodily form like a dove upon Him, and a voice came from heaven which*

*said, "You are My beloved Son; in You I am well pleased."*
*—Luke 3:21-22*

In all these passages, we see the threefold expression of God, and the Holy Spirit's part as God. We also see Him addressed as a personality and not an "it." I hear people, all the time, addressing the Holy Spirit as an it or a mystical ghostly mist. He is the third person of the trinity. He is God and should be honored as so. Take the time to listen, intently, to what Jesus was saying about the Holy Spirit in His teaching the disciples.

*And I will pray the Father, and He will give you another Helper, that He may abide with you forever—the Spirit of truth, whom the world cannot receive, because it neither sees Him nor knows Him; but you know Him, for He dwells with you and will be in you.*
*—John 14:16-17*

## The Role of the Holy Spirit

In the passage above, we see Jesus talk about the person whom He is going to send to be another Helper. This meant another one like Him. This person was going to come alongside them and fulfill the role that Christ had had in their lives, up until that point. This is so very important. Jesus made it clear that He was not going to leave them orphans or unprepared to fulfill the Great Commission. He was giving them everything they needed to be successful as abiding leaders.

The Greek word that is used for "helper" here is

*paraklētos*. This word is translated as "comforter," "counselor," "advocate," "intercessor," "strengthener," "standby," or "helper."[25] That sure sounds encouraging to me. Who would not want all the things that the word implies? Don't you think Jesus knew what He was doing? He was not making a mistake when He taught them this. If you are going to abide, and lead an abiding Church, you must understand the importance of what Jesus was instituting here.

> *These things I have spoken to you while being present with you. But the Helper, the Holy Spirit, whom the Father will send in My name, He will teach you all things, and bring to your remembrance all things that I said to you.*
>
> **—John 14:25–26**

> *What no eye has seen, nor ear heard, nor the heart of man imagined, what God has prepared for those who love him—these things God has revealed to us through the Spirit. For the Spirit searches everything, even the depths of God. For who knows a person's thoughts except the spirit of that person, which is in him? So also no one comprehends the thoughts of God except the Spirit of God. Now we have received not the spirit of the world, but the Spirit who is from God, that we might understand the things freely given us by God. And we impart this in words not taught by human wisdom but taught by the Spirit, interpreting spiritual truths to those who are spiritual.*
>
> **—1 Corinthians 2:9–13** *(ESV)*

I love the thought here. Jesus was reminding them that there is so much more that He could not cram into the brief time He was with them, but that it was okay. He was giving them more than an answer book. He was giving them the answer. He was giving them the key to staying connected to the vine. He was giving them the way to abide, the Holy Spirit.

Remember, we discussed, in earlier chapters, that most programs and Bible studies give you specific tools and steps for specific scenarios. This can be good, but what happens when you come up against something you never studied for? When your training did not include the answers to your current crisis? Jesus gave you something so much better. He gave you the answer, the Holy Spirit. The Abiding Church relies less on the operating principles, but the empowerment of the direct voice of the Holy Spirit to lead and guide. How awesome is this?

He desires to direct our path, according to His righteousness. Too many Christians write off the responsibility that God gives us to hear His voice. They claim that, if it's really God's will, then He will make it happen. An abider in Christ will hear His voice and obey.

There are things that God wants to reveal to you, but they have to happen through spiritual discernment. We can know the mind of Christ and follow His blueprint with clarity by leaning into this relationship as a part of our abiding. What an amazing gift God has given us in the Holy Spirit. If you are not looking for this relationship, then you could pass Him by every day of your life and miss what God is wanting to reveal to you.

*Likewise, the Spirit also helps in our weaknesses. For we*

*do not know what we should pray for as we ought, but the Spirit Himself makes intercession for us with groanings which cannot be uttered. Now He who searches the hearts knows what the mind of the Spirit is, because He makes intercession for the saints according to the will of God. And we know that all things work together for good to those who love God, to those who are the called according to His purpose.*

**—Romans 8:26–28**

These verses remind us that God has a purpose and destiny for us that will work out for our good. The Holy Spirit will help us to pray and find that out. He intercedes on our behalf and can help us to pray. Prayer is such an important part of abiding in Christ. The more you abide, the less you come to God with petitions. The more you abide, the more you come to Him, simply to be in His presence and remain in Him. You learn to let Him take care of the needs and petitions that used to worry you. You understand that He promised to take care of the everyday needs, and He simply wants to abide with you.

## *A Powerful Prayer Life*

*But you shall receive power when the Holy Spirit has come upon you; and you shall be witnesses to Me in Jerusalem, and in all Judea and Samaria, and to the end of the earth.*

**—Acts 1:8**

I am not sure about you, but I need daily power to live a successful walk with Christ. There is so much sin and depravity in our world that I simply don't have the tools to overcome, in my human ability, let alone lead others. Jesus made provision for that, as well. The verse above is one of the last recorded statements that Jesus made. He told His followers that there was more to learn.

> Behold, I send the Promise of My Father upon you; but tarry in the city of Jerusalem until you are endued with power from on high.
> —**Luke 24:49**

Jesus was saying, "You need what I am giving, and you are going to love Him." The Greek word translated to "power" is *dunamis*. The definition is "force," "miraculous power," "ability," "abundance," "might," "power," or "strength."[26]

So, what does this mean in practice? How do we move forward into a new, abiding relationship with God as an empowered Church leader?

## 1. Experience Who God Is

As a disciple of Christ, you should find a way to experience Christ every day. This can happen in a time of prayer, worship, church service, devotion, or a whole host of ways. It should not be limited to a time frame set apart in your day. You should learn to experience Him all day every day. To abide in Christ takes a big commitment. There are many things fighting for your time, and the tyranny of the urgent usually wins out. You must make Him a priority, including Him into every part of your day. Remember that Christ should be the center of your life instead of just at the top of a list for the day.

If I only spoke to my wife once a week at church, our relationship would become strained over time. I would have stopped experiencing her. In much the same way, many Christians think they can only experience Christ once a week in an hour-long church service and have an abiding relationship with Him. This limited time will slowly stress the relationship. You will quit abiding in Him and only go to Him on your terms when you want something. You will quit hearing His leadings, and His blueprint will slowly fade away until you are living your life for you again. This is a slippery slope that many Christians find themselves on.

As we have already addressed in this book, many Church leaders put so much emphasis on a once-a-week corporate gathering that it hinders a vision for members to pursue discipleship. I read an article this week from a nationally known Church leader with a large church. The entire article touted that everything we do as Christians should builds toward Sunday and that Sunday was the most important day of the week. I was pretty taken aback at the lack of biblical wisdom that was being shared as truth in this article. The Abiding Church model teaches the opposite of that. Sunday, or corporate gathering times, are biblical, necessary, and can be a great encouragement to our faith. However, when you abide in Christ, you should live in intimacy with Christ every day. You don't need Sunday to experience God. An Abiding Church will put the focus of experiencing God into many contexts and not limit it to a once-a-week corporate gathering.

Make your drive to work a time of abiding.
Acknowledge Christ in your work and make your work
worship to Him. Washing dishes can be a time of worship and communion with Him. Folding laundry can be
surrounded with the presence of God. Are you getting it
now? Make it a commitment to experience Him all day,
every day.

## 2. Discover and Grow in the Gifts God Has Given You

This part of the process involves discovery and growing in every way possible. As you experience God, you
will discover who God is and who you are in relationship
with Him. Discover what He has created you for and
your purpose as He unfolds it to you over the next seasons of your life. Grow in the gifts that God has given
you. Grow in fellowship with Him. Grow in the
knowledge of the Word. Grow in your faith. Grow in His
love for you. Every day you should find practical ways
to develop in your relationship with God.

This could involve a daily Bible study, a church discipleship class, leading your family in devotions, or
many other things. The more you can learn about God
and the Bible, the more He can grow you and lead you
according to His will. This has to happen alongside experiencing Him. You don't want to gain knowledge
without relationship. However, when the two work hand
in hand, you will see God reveal things to you that you
never comprehended before. So many believers find
Christ and let Him be their Savior, providing them with

an escape from hell. Then they stop there and don't pursue allowing God to be their Lord. There is a big difference. When Christ is your Lord, you are growing every day in personal abandonment and absolute trust in Him. You experience eternal life here and now and not just in heaven.

> *But grow in grace, and in the knowledge of our Lord and Savior Jesus Christ. To him be glory both now and forever. Amen.*
> —*2 Peter 3:18*

## 3. Share the Love of Christ in Practical Ways

When you experience and grow in God every day, sharing Him will be a natural outflow of your life. You will find ways to share His love with people in your area of influence. There are people whom God has placed in your life who may never hear the message of Christ outside of you sharing it with them. This is a responsibility and a privilege. Remember, your life is about bringing glory to God. What better way to bring Him glory than to share your story of how God's love transformed your life and how He can do the same for others?

I have heard of some Church leaders teaching their churches that their role is to simply invite people to church. Then the job of the pastors is to get the people saved. Huh? This is why so many churches center their services around the altar call. Their culture assumes that this corporate gathering and this pastor are the only ways God can move on the unsaved and bring them to salvation.

Once again, what does the Bible say to this? The Abiding Church model helps people realize that part of your role as a Christian is to be on a mission in your sphere of influence. You have gifts, the Holy Spirit, and the Word of God, and you can do the work of the ministry just like anyone else. The problem is that too many are not abiding in Christ and having a daily experience with Him. They have not been discipled or grown in their journey with Christ and so they are not equipped to share the love of Christ.

God will give you divine appointments with people and open doors to simply talk about Him. You can use this process to share His love. It's less about Scriptures and theology and more about letting them know that God loves them and wants to be in relationship with them. I want to warn you, though, that sharing the love of Christ becomes addictive. When you share His love, and someone comes to know Him, it is the most awesome experience on earth. Heaven rejoices, and you get more excited to share Him with even more people.

WORKBOOK

# Chapter Eleven Questions

**Question:** Describe the role of the Holy Spirit in your life. How do walking in the Spirit and abiding in Christ go hand in hand?

_____

_____

_____

_____

_____

_____

_____

_____

_____

_____

_____

**Question:** How do you "experience Christ" on a daily basis? How can spiritual disciplines aid you in this?

_____

_____

_____

_____

_____

_____

_____

_____

_____

_____

**Action:** Ask the Holy Spirit to lead you in beginning a new or neglected spiritual discipline (such as fasting, silence and solitude, or early rising). After one week, evaluate whether or not this has helped you grow and abide.

**Journal:** Follow the STAR method for Habakkuk 2:1–4

## *Chapter Eleven Notes*

_____

_____

_____

_____

_____

_____

_____

_____

_____

_____

_____

_____

_____

_____

_____

_____

_____

_____

_____

_____

_____

_____

_____

# Becoming an Abiding Church

You have an amazing road ahead as you prayerfully explore and navigate your individual and organizational blueprint from God. This chapter lays out some basic principles that can be a catalyst to help you develop your blueprint.

My intention is to draw out of you by the power of the Holy Spirit your specific callings and giftings. You are a gift from God to the body of Christ, and I want to see you produce Kingdom fruit where you are planted.

Serving as a leader in a local expression of the body of Christ, I have discovered some key ingredients that make for a healthy biblical community. Following is a list of these ingredients that can serve as the foundation for an Abiding Church model.

That said, each local expression of the body of Christ will have unique ways and forms in which these are lived out. It is vitally important that you and your leadership take the time to seek the Lord and allow Him to define what this looks like for your church. We want you to walk out your unique, God-given blueprint, rather than merely copying what someone else does.

## Seven Characteristics of a Healthy Biblical Community

Identity is vitally important to living in the fullness that God has for you. If you are unsure of who you are, then you will have a hard time fulfilling your purpose. As a church leader, you should desire that the individuals you lead would discover who they are in Christ and why He created them. You also should want your church body to know why the Church exists, in a universal sense as well as in your local context.

You should develop a clear vision that all members can commit to and follow. Everyone has expectations in all areas of life, and when our experience does not align with our expectations, there is an open door for broken relationship and offense. The seven characteristics of a healthy biblical community can help define your expectations of your church members and leaders as well as clarify what they can expect from your leadership.

I am going to use the wording that I put in place in the local context of Catalyst Church in Bentonville, Arkansas. This concrete example may help you understand these points more clearly. It may also spark some thought into how you can create, implement, and cultivate these seven principles in your local church context. Each principle encompasses much more information and detail than is presented here and requires much prayerful consideration.

At the time of publishing this revised edition, I have worked with over four hundred church leaders, in many different contexts, to help them implement some of these principles. There are many different God-breathed ways to fulfill biblical discipleship, and I want to encourage you to prayerfully discover how God is leading you, specifically. The Abiding Church begins with abiding leaders, connected to the vine and walking in obedience to the Father's directives.

If something here sparks your interest in further discussion, you may consider reaching out for encouragement and mentorship to another leader at an Abiding Church. There are many resources available on your journey that will be relevant in each step of the process. You can find out more at www.abidingnetwork.com.

## 1. Clearly Defined Vision

Vision is the act or power of anticipating that which will or may come. Vision gives us the ability to see things not as they are, but how God sees them. Vision helps us align everything we do toward a singular focus. Vision helps us look beyond the state we are in to see what God can transform it into. This includes people, process of ministry, organizational principles, and so much more. We apply everything we do under the vision. We want our vision to propel us into all that God has for us as a church and as individuals.

In all simplicity, Christ is in charge. It's His Church.

He is the real Senior Pastor. He has the plan. He gives it to His Church. We humbly receive, submit to, and obey His plan as servants and oversee His directives. We are stewards of His Church.

> *Where there is no vision, the people cast off restraint [become undisciplined and disobedient].*
> **—Proverbs 29:18a** *(ASV)*

> *Where there is no vision, the people are uncontrolled.*
> **—Proverbs 29:18a** *(BBE)*

> *Where there is no vision, the people perish.*
> **—Proverbs 29:18a** *(KJV)*

As you spend time in church and around the church world, there seems to be a tendency to complicate things. Many Christians fall into a trap that "more is better." Many will try to convince you that you need "Christ and [fill-in the-blank]." They will try to add things on top of Christ for your salvation. Many of these people are good-hearted but can lead you astray from abiding in Christ.

Jesus kept things very simple and spoke practically to people. So many times, the simplicity of Christ's method is overlooked as "too easy." People think that there must be more to this, so they say, "Give me something to do and I'll do it." Do not lose fellowship *with* Him in your pursuit to know *about* Him. The most important thing moving forward is your abiding in Him. Abiding in Christ should never be bypassed in your pursuit to gain knowledge about God. There is a big difference, but it is easy to fall into this trap.

We hope the vision God has given to us is clear and concise. We want you to take ownership of this vision and make it yours. Don't simply attend Catalyst Church. Take on the identity of being a catalyst for Christ. Our vision is: "Knowing Christ and Making Him Known."

## 2. Clearly Defined Process of Making Disciples

The hardest part of discipleship with people is walking with them on their journey through brokenness. Discipleship is messy, costly, inefficient, and time-consuming. Everyone travels on his or her journey at his or her own pace. Learning to walk with people on this journey with grace, truth, accountability, and patience is a work of the Holy Spirit—and very difficult on the soul.

The greatest joy in my leadership life has been walking with people on their transformation journeys toward intimacy with Christ. This is what makes all the investment so rewarding. When people finally get it, and they walk in their God-given blueprint, you're reminded that this is why you do what you do. Life transformation is the greatest measurable when leading people in discipleship.

What is the role of the church leadership in discipleship? To connect the head to the body. To help people get into proximity with Christ and, eventually, into an intimate, abiding relationship with Him. To equip the saints to do the work of the ministry. To make disciples by helping develop members spiritually and releasing them into their areas of gifting and influence. This includes reproduction, mentoring, and becoming spiritual fathers and mothers to new believers.

*As long as a church leadership team creates a platform for discipleship that engages the heart of individuals leading to transformation, then the form of what you do is less important.* When you lose the power of transformation in a spiritual community, you quickly revert to religious activity to stay alive. If you have a lot of religious activity in your church, but are not seeing heart transformation, then maybe the form you are using is not founded in the function of biblical discipleship. Religious churches rely on organization to rally people and eventually become institutionalized. An institution will eventually become a museum of what it once was.

This characteristic will help you define and share how your church will fulfill, or "put hands and feet," to the vision. It helps pattern programs and events in such a way that they stay focused on the vision while being a catalyst in people's lives to help them in their daily walk with Christ. This process is not a system of achievement, but rather a continual awareness that will help promote Christ. At any given time, our church members should be able to acknowledge the ministry process in their worship, fellowship, spiritual development, and service.

## 3. Clearly Defined Training Center

Many churches are only teaching centers where people come to learn. In addition to teaching, however, the Bible calls the Church to be a training center, equipping people to do the work of the ministry. If I am just a teacher and you are just a student, that means you will always be the student. You will always be acquiring more knowledge (and nothing more).

A training center says that at some point, you are going to be held responsible—and not merely on a quiz or a test. You will be called on to live out what you have learned. You will need to be able to apply this learned knowledge practically in your daily discipleship journey. Someone who is trained is a disciple and has hands-on experience with the knowledge he or she has been taught. This then empowers the disciple to lead others. Disciples are faithful people who can teach and train others also. As a disciple, you are a pupil, a follower, a learner, a teacher, and a trainer. But, what does this look like?

Teaching centers have become the norm for many mainline churches in America today. The idea is: "Come here to get taught and be sent back out." Teaching centers focus on knowledge transfer. Teaching centers focus on large-group settings and crowd size. Teaching centers focus little on care and discipleship. Teaching centers hire trained leaders that manage large groups. Teaching centers have a few ministers doing most of the work of the ministry. Teaching centers offer menus of learning opportunities.

We need to realign our churches to be teaching and training centers. Training centers focus on knowledge *and* on skills to be exercised in applying that knowledge.

Training centers offer hands-on discipleship environments that are accountable, as well as mentoring and spiritual parenting. Training centers focus on care and discipleship. Training centers raise up leaders and release them into ministry. Training centers empower people in ministry because they value the biblical understanding that *all are ministers*. Training centers offer personalized maps for each person to navigate his or her journey within the context of the local body.

Many churches offer a great assimilation plan, but it stops there. They neglect to offer a long-term platform of discipleship that offers accountability and training for biblical transformation.

Assimilation is a plan that comprises steps needed to absorb an individual or family into the larger body or biblical community of the Church. This must be intentionally organic and requires the right plan as well as the leadership to work that plan.

Discipleship Growth Tracks are individual plans of growth for each person within the organization or church. This can be accompanied by a Church-based training center or outside sources. It must be led by a mentor or leader who helps walk with this person for accountability, encouragement, and empowerment.

Some characteristics of a church-based growth track could be as follows:

**Informative and transformative.** We want to give you the knowledge to confidently know Christ and then connect with intimacy in Him so you can become transformed into His image. Transformed (not conformed) lives are the greatest measurable that we have found in stewarding discipleship opportunities.

**New born.** We place huge significance on new birth within each growth track, as we should. However, fully-formed disciples grow much further beyond the new birth. We want to help facilitate your spiritual growth beyond your new birth.

**Spiritual development.** Most churches put some importance on this but offer little direction and leadership in developing spiritually. It is mostly left up to the individual to figure that out. However, we want to change this cultural norm and get you on a track to develop fully in your spiritual journey with Christ.

**Discovery and empowerment into ministry.** We want to help you discover who God is, who you are in relationship to this God, and then why He created you and put you here on earth. This process incorporates your personality and your God-given gifts, talents, and passions. We want to align each of these with your calling to see you step into all God has for you.

**Practical growth strategies.** The abovementioned discovery and empowerment open the door to practical growth strategies that are personalized for you. We walk with you on your journey of discipleship based on what you have discovered from God about your specific mix of calling and gift.

**Vision and passion.** Growth produces a hunger to be shaped and built into your God-breathed blueprint. When you discover your passion and are given the tools to walk it out effectively, there is nothing else like it. Ministry is no longer work because you are empowered by the Holy Spirit to function as God created you. This passion will become a driver that motivates your growth.

**Reproduction.** A mature and fully formed disciple will reproduce. You should be able to take what God has done in you and teach/train other people whom He places in your sphere of influence.

If you want to have an Abiding Church, you will at some point need to find a way to make disciples in a context that works in your leadership culture. This takes intentionality, vision, strategy, discipline, and empowerment. This is not something that I think most churches' organizational structures can handle. It takes a lot of administrative and leadership resources and does not happen in the context of a large once a week corporate gathering.

Using available online resources, find a good program that you can customize and utilize to help people take steps along their individual tracks. The best foundational tool I have found is something called the Influencer's Journey (see www.influencers.org). Our ministry growth track, teaching programs, and Sunday sermons all use the Journey as a cultural touchstone and foundation. If you want to be in a long-term leadership role at Catalyst, the Journey is part of your development.

This also helps us bring continuity to our membership. When most of our body has been through this same process, there is a unity of the Spirit that I have not seen before. God has used this journey to revolutionize our biblical community and many others on a global scale (see Further Resources).

Here is a general outline that we have put in place at Catalyst Church for personal growth tracks.

***Student assessment with a coach or mentor.*** We start each growth track with a simple assessment with a coach, pastor, mentor, Catalyst Group leader, or whomever is leading you, the disciple in training. We use what we call the Abiding Leader Profile. This consists of some key areas on which we want to focus in your next season. This track is personally designed for each person, so we don't set the agenda. We allow the Holy Spirit to lead each step of the process as we challenge you and hold you accountable. We want this profile to help you examine your own calling, gifts, and passions and to align those things with the training you need to fully walk out God's plan for your life.

***Soul health.*** How is your soul? Most people admit that no one has ever asked them this question. We want this assessment to help you answer that question honestly and then create a track for you to live in soul health.

***Relationships.*** Look around at your relationships: marriage, friendships, family, and leadership. What is the health of your relationships? What do you need to bring health to these key areas? Add these things to your track.

***Personal theology.*** I have been disappointed over the years when I sit with people who seem to be spiritually healthy, only to find that they merely have a lot of knowledge about the Bible. This does not necessarily equate to spiritual health. The key is to learn how to live out that biblical knowledge with faith and obedience and skillfully apply it to your life.

***Hurts, habits, hang-ups.*** Every one of us has dysfunction somewhere in our lives. It may be so hidden that we are blind to it, but God wants us to be free from

them. A growth track is the perfect environment and creates a safe place to process these issues. We talk about
dysfunction as land mines. Imagine if you stepped on
one of these land mines in your life? What would the
collateral damage be to all of the other areas of your life?
This area is one that most people don't realize they need
to face, but in growth tracks they end up realizing and
addressing these challenges.

*Personality assessment.* How did God wire you? We
have found that when we do personality assessments
with people, the discovery process is a huge encouragement for them. Discovering how God created you and
others can help you live with a grace and language of
communication that will foster healthy relationships.
This portion of the growth track has revolutionized many
lives!

*Spiritual gift assessment.* How did God gift you?
This piggybacks off of the personality assessment.

*Personal growth track.* At this point of the assessment, we simply ask you if you want to commit to this
process. If you say "Yes," we begin the "next steps"
conversation. We introduce you to the Journey. We show
you the massive list of classes and books in our training
library that you need to prayerfully consider adding to
your long-term personal track. We want you to see this
as a marathon, not a sprint. Each person's growth track
will move at the pace he or she is able to sustain. We do
not impose parameters based on what we want, but we
do offer input and leadership advice. Ultimately, we
want people to own their personal discipleship journey.
We want you to learn to self-feed in a vertical, intimate

relationship with Christ. We then set our next meeting date, time, and agenda.

*5 Es of leadership development* (see Appendix A). The last part of the assessment is explaining the 5 Es process of leadership development. We have used the 5 Es across several ministry and leadership platforms for many years—and it works. We want people to see that this process takes lots of work, planning, strategy, discipline, intentionality, and humility. If you want to become all God has for you in this discipleship journey, then there needs to be a plan, and the 5 Es lay that out.

We do not require you to be on a growth track to be a member of Catalyst Church. We simply ask that you let God lead you into what is next for you as you abide in Him. No matter what is next for you, we want it to be what God has called *you* to do.

## 4. Clearly Defined Biblical Doctrines

Do the people sitting in your pews each week know the truth? Could they tell the difference between clear biblical doctrine and some preacher's soap box? If asked, could they defend the faith that they are counting on for their eternal security? Deception is very difficult to see if you are not grounded in the truth. There are many counterfeits in this world, and we want you to have the truth of God so you can live it out and see fruit in your life.

At Catalyst Church, we use terms like *primary, secondary, closed hand,* and *open hand* to define doctrine versus theology. Primary, close-handed issues are what I would describe as doctrine. Doctrine is biblically settled, and we don't get to change that. It is to be accepted, learned, and digested as you grow in your walk with Christ.

*Secondary* and *open-handed* are how I would describe theology. Theology is defined as the study of God. These are biblical or even cultural ideas that can be seen in different ways through Scripture, depending on each individual's personal journey, cultural, and historical context. Doctrine should be lived out through fellowship with God and is not dependent on experience, while open-handed topics are not salvation-dependent beliefs and are unique to each person story.

It's important for your church members to know what doctrine they believe. This should be preached clearly and regularly. Primary beliefs should be the filter through which everything is viewed. When your entire church knows these and is able to explain them, you have a stronger church.

## 5. Clearly Defined Gospel-Centered Teaching

> *For I am not ashamed of the gospel of Christ, for it is the power of God to salvation for everyone who believes, for the Jew first and also for the Greek. For in it the righteousness of God is revealed from faith to faith; as it is written, "The just shall live by faith."*
> **—Romans 1:16–17**

This gospel message is so vital to the Church today. It is this message in which the righteousness of God is revealed. We must be careful to keep this at the forefront, as the main thing. We covered this in detail in chapter 10, so I'll only add a few notes here.

## Assumptions

One set of assumptions we typically make as church leaders is that people in our sphere of influence have the same value system and moral standards that we have. We assume everyone in our church is on the same page as to what defines sin, grace, obedience, and holiness. However, in my experience as a church leader, I have come to understand that we are not all automatically on the same page within the context of our church.

*There is a preexisting, understood consensus about what sin is, about what is right and what is wrong. There is preexisting consensus relative to what grace looks like in practical daily living. There is preexisting consensus relative to what holiness is and whether we would embrace holiness if we were to fully recognize it.* We cannot afford to assume that any of these statements is true.

America is no longer predominantly Christian in its worldview. I see America more as a church at Syria and Antioch. These were Gentile strongholds in which Paul preached the gospel and saw lives brought from the bondage of sin to transformation in Christ. He preached sin, grace, obedience, and holiness. As the American mainstream becomes more secular in character, we must find balance in our gospel declaration and neither become legalistic nor water down the gospel truth and keep people from the true Kingdom.

## 6. Biblical Community with Clearly Defined Cultural Core Values

Every biblical community or expression of the body of Christ will have unique methods and vision to fulfill the call to make disciples. One definition of *culture* is the "behaviors and belief characteristics of a particular social group."[27]

Every church or ministry has a culture; some proactively create and define culture while others allow culture to be defined by whatever experiences come along. If you want to become an Abiding Church, you will want to spend time examining the core values of your church.

We need a clearly defined biblical community that offers accountability, shared experiences, and biblically defined membership, and that promotes doing life together.

In this regard, let me speak for a moment about the power of expectations. We all have expectations for our churches based on many things, such as past experiences, denominational leanings, and personal preferences. What do you expect from a church? What do you expect from a church leadership? What do you expect from a church member?

No church family is perfect. If you find one that seems that way, don't attend—because you will mess it all up! Churches are made up of individuals working out their salvation, and therefore they are all flawed. You will get hurt at church. People will fail you, and you will fail them.

Over the years we have witnessed people with unhealthy and unrealistic expectations. We have also had seasons when we as a church have done a poor job in clarifying expectations. Many times, this has led to relationship breakdown and parting of ways. We want you to flourish in the vineyard in which God plants you.

Here are ten core values that have become part of our healthy church culture:

**Abiding in Christ**. We intentionally and continually point people to an intimate, abiding relationship with Christ. *We understand that staying connected to the vine of Christ is our life and that without this, we can do nothing of eternal significance. This connection produces Kingdom fruit by which Father God is glorified.*

**Accountability** is a willingness to be challenged and accept personal responsibility. *We understand that God did not create us to live in isolation. Part of our DNA as humans is to be in community. At Catalyst Church, we promote biblical accountability, which considers one another in order to stir up love and good works.*

We are all under authority in different areas of our lives. We are first accountable to God, and then to our civil authorities, bosses, and one another. At Catalyst, we want everyone to embrace and learn to appreciate accountability. A healthy believer has others in his sphere of influence who will hold him or her accountable to the Word of God in behavior, attitude, and many other areas. A person who avoids accountability opens himself or herself up to making wrong decisions.

**Authenticity** is genuine transparency. *We understand*

*that to have a healthy spiritual community, we must cre-*
*ate a culture that promotes genuineness and*
*transparency. Catalyst Church is a safe place to fall,*
*heal, grow, be empowered, and simply be who God cre-*
*ated you to be.*

People can smell a fake coming from miles away. In
ministry, it is so important that we lead from a place of
sincerity and transparency. One characteristic of our society today is that people want to relate. If people cannot
relate to us or feel we relate to them, they will not follow. We have to be confident enough in our abiding
relationship with Christ that we can show our weakness,
struggles, and fears in an effort to grow into who God
created us to be. Authentic people bring credibility to the
conversation and a leadership style that others do not
have. If people can see you're a work in progress, too, it
gives them hope. To have healthy relationships, they
must exist in a culture that promotes genuineness, authenticity, and transparency.

**Discipleship** is producing fully-devoted followers of
Christ. *We understand Christ's command to make disci-*
*ples, and we take it seriously. Discipleship is one of the*
*main focuses at Catalyst Church. A healthy church cul-*
*ture will consist of disciples making disciples and*
*fulfilling the Great Commission.*

**Diversity**. We celebrate God's diverse and unique
creation within the larger body of Christ. *We understand*
*that God has created us all in His image, yet with indi-*
*vidual uniqueness. In love, we place value on people*
*from all walks of life, including history, age, race, per-*
*sonality, social/economic background, denomination,*

*and giftedness.*

**Empowerment**. We are called to empower people to move into their Christ-given callings. *We understand that God has called all of us to minister with the gifts He has placed on our lives. Our spiritual community is a great place to be empowered to discover, grow in, and minister with the gifts God has given each person.*

**Generosity**. We are faithful stewards who are generous with our time, treasure, and talents. *We understand that God is a very generous Father and desires us to extend that generosity to others. A healthy church should consist of people who have freely received from God and freely give to others.*

**Love** is demonstrated in the balance of grace and truth. *We understand love to be a perfect balance of grace and truth and strive to magnify that.* Love is the perfect balance of two virtues that cannot be balanced. We should have community that displays the grace and truth we want others to display to us. God does not deal harshly with us, but rather leads us with grace and truth. This can be a challenging struggle at times but is never characterized by domineering or abusive treatment. If God leads us this way, then we should lead others with the same DNA. Truth can be confrontational and difficult at times but should always be seasoned with grace.

**Transformation**. For the Christian, transformation means being changed into the image of Christ. *We understand that we cannot change or fix anyone, so we don't try to conform people to our image or ways of doing things. Our goal is to be a catalyst to get you close to Christ and allow Him to transform your life and change* *you into His image.*

**Trust**. By trust, I mean absolute trust in God and in one another. *We understand that personal abandonment and absolute trust in God are essential to live in faith. We extend this trust to include trusting others in the family of God as we strive to walk in love with others.*

Trust is a virtue that seems to be lost in this generation. So many of the people and institutions that have held our trust in years past have let us down: parents, religious leaders, government, education systems—and the list could go on. In the Kingdom of God, we need to learn, through love and faith, to develop trust with one another. As we grow in spiritual community, trust is something that will be earned and valued. Trust is the foundation for so many other things that we could miss out on if we neglect this core value.

## 7. Clearly Defined Biblical Leadership Roles

There are many modern-day models that fit under the clear biblical leadership roles of governance, duplication, and reproduction that we could explore. For the sake of space, I will limit much of what I could add in this section. The important takeaway from this characteristic is that your leadership finds the model that God desires for your local expression.

At Catalyst Church, we have chosen an elder-led governance model that includes a mosaic of many modern-day models. This allows our leaders to be empowered and work in their gifts and calling.

In my experience, not having this characteristic defined has caused so much leadership pain and stunted church health and ultimate growth. Getting this characteristic in place and functioning will be a huge catalyst in making transitions into an Abiding Church.

# Chapter Twelve Questions

**Question:** Look at the seven characteristics of a healthy biblical community. In which areas is your church strong? In which areas do you seek to improve and how? What additional characteristics, if any, could you acknowledge for your local expression of biblical community?

_____

_____

_____

_____

_____

_____

_____

_____

**Question:** The clearly defined vision could also be called a mission statement. Does your church's mission statement also convey its vision?

_____

_____

_____

_____

_____

_____

_____

_____

_____

_____

**Action:** Each of the seven characteristics begins with the words "Clearly defined." How is your church doing in clear communication? How can your church improve in making your message more clear and understandable? If this is a struggle, consider reading a book, taking a course, or seeking a mentor to assist. Consult the www.abidingnetwork.com website for ideas, inspiration, or further conversation.

# *Chapter Twelve Notes*

_____

_____

_____

_____

_____

_____

_____

_____

_____

_____

_____

_____

_____

_____

_____

_____

_____

_____

_____

_____

_____

_____

CONCLUSION

# Closing Thoughts

Before you run off and start making any major changes, I want to offer some last bits of advice. If you become an Abiding Church, you will experience great amounts of Kingdom fruit. It makes your roles so much more satisfying when you see this fruit begin to come to pass.

It can be a good thing to create an organizational chart to clearly communicate everyone's specific role. It is also good to learn how to implement strategic planning into your governance oversight. Years ago, we learned and implemented a simple model called 5-2-1 Strategic Leadership Planning, which we pulled from another local church. This has been a joy to walk out as we implement these strategic leadership pieces.

The 5-2-1 is a model that helps you identify long-term dreams and put them into a short-term clarified plan of action for your organization.

The 5 is a five-year dream space. At any time, our eldership may have a dozen or more dream conversations that we talk about in the abstract. We dream about what God may be leading us to do.

The 2 is when we take a five-year dream space topic and put it in a two-year funnel. This funnel helps us to strategically pray, think, read, and discuss many things around this dream. For example: If we implemented this dream, would it advance our vision and mission? What are the risks and rewards associated with this dream? What would it take organizationally to get our oars in the water and start rowing? After we have thoroughly processed this portion of the dream, we can either put it back in the dream space or move it to a one-year plan.

The 1 represents a one-year plan of action and implementation. It comes with a lot of programs, budgets, job description updates, and other practical details.

It is a good thing to ask others outside to help you on your journey. Don't hesitate to get into a network of like-minded local churches and let the relationships sharpen one another. This is not a competition. We are all on the same team. Learn to humbly, freely receive and freely give to others.

You may be in a season when you need to establish some new things. You may need to relaunch some things. You may simply need to expand on some areas in which you are doing well. And you may need to start over completely in other areas. Wherever you are, be a prayer-centered church. Submit all the knowledge in this book to the Lord. Allow your leadership culture to be bathed in prayer. An Abiding Church will see prayer as exciting as you draw near to Christ individually and corporately. There should be a unity of the Spirit that saturates the DNA of your leadership and congregation.

Are you desiring to plant a garden or an orchard? Most gardens are planted with the intention of quick harvest and with the knowledge that you will need to do it all again next season. An orchard is planted with a long-term, sustainable vision in place. Orchards take many years to develop and see fruit. However, orchards will continue to produce fruit for decades and possibly centuries. Either way, we want a Kingdom harvest.

Consider the cost so that you can complete what you start. It will cost you to make changes that will move you toward becoming an Abiding Church. When I started on my journey years ago, we lost half of our members within the first six months of applying these principles. It was a very healthy season as we relaunched with a new focus. If we had been hung up on unhealthy measurements, we would have stopped in the middle and done something different. In other recent seasons, we have seen tremendous health through seasons of pruning as a church.

Whatever God leads you to do will take time. Too many Church leaders I have discipled do not want to patiently walk out the process of becoming an Abiding Church. Many simply want a conference style, a new drive-through formula that will be easy and fast. They want to plant a garden and see a quick harvest instead of taking the time necessary to plant orchards. The amount of investment work can typically end up being the same, but one begins to multiply as the years go on while the other needs constant replanting each season. In my experience, there are no shortcuts for discipleship. Spiritual fruit can take years to develop. Many times, it begins with a handful of transformed lives that add up into dozens and eventually multiplies into many more. The foundation may be the longest part of this process, so don't build on it before it has time to cure. Too many leaders give it six months and then jump ship to another process without giving this time to cultivate and produce.

Learn to keep it simple and say no to almost everything extraneous. One danger occurs when we want to take the knowledge we have learned and run with it all before we are ready. Simplicity is a key to healthy organizations. Learn to strategically put things in place in as simple of a process and time frame as possible. Remember, earlier in this book we said that more complicated does not equate to more spiritual. Some of the best ideas and plans are timeless and simple. Don't overcomplicate any part of this process. Christ did not do that, so we can use His example for our benefit.

Finally, remember to keep a vibrant relationship with Christ at the center of it all. When you abide in Him, your life will produce fruit, and an Abiding Church will leave a mark on this world for the glory of God.

WORKBOOK

# Conclusion Questions

**Question:** What do you perceive to be the costs—to you, as well as your church—of becoming an Abiding Church versus a consumer church?

_____

_____

_____

_____

_____

_____

_____

_____

_____

_____

**Action:** Making changes within a church takes time, patience, and organization. Thinking back over this book, list the changes you would like to facilitate, in order of importance. Then write out a plan and a timeline to implement each change.

**Journal:** Think through the ideas that have stood out the most to you from this book. Journal about them and your commitment to being an abiding believer and an Abiding Church.

APPENDIX A

# The Five Es of Leadership Development

In my opinion, good leaders understand that their influence matters. They take the time to discover their gifts and callings. They invest in learning how to skillfully manage their own leadership, and then they apply that into their sphere of influence. Good leaders are self-aware and are in a constant state of growth. Good leaders get a lot of work accomplished and excel wherever they are planted.

Great leaders, on the other hand, realize somewhere in their leadership that there is more joy in empowering others than doing the work themselves. Great leaders understand that they have strengths and weaknesses and they address both. They learn to cultivate an environment where their particular giftings can be passionately used to propel the organization ahead.

*But I trust in the Lord Jesus to send Timothy to you short-*

*ly, that I also may be encouraged when I know your state. For I have no one like-minded, who will sincerely care for your state. For all seek their own, not the things which are of Christ Jesus. But you know his proven character, that as a son with his father he served with me in the gospel.*
*—Philippians 2:19–22*

*You therefore, my son, be strong in the grace that is in Christ Jesus. And the things that you have heard from me among many witnesses, commit these to faithful men who will be able to teach others also.*
*—2 Timothy 2:1–2*

As godly leaders and disciples of Christ, part of our DNA should be to produce leaders around us. Developing a leader helps that person become who God has created them to be. Great leaders don't wake up one day where they are. They had people speak into their life and give them a chance to learn, fail, develop, and succeed. Someone saw something in you when you were still raw, and we should turn around and do the same. A great leader understands that he has been given a task that is so much larger than him. A great leader will rise up and empower people around him to help him accomplish God's vision.

In the Bible, we see many great examples of leadership development from which we can learn and teach. These principles are universal and can be used in business, family, church life, and anywhere God is giving you influence. I have chosen to break some of these principles down into what we call the Five Es of Leadership Development.

## 1. Establish

As a leader, it is your job to prayerfully put into place the things that God is leading you toward, in your direct areas of oversight. This includes the long-term task of developing a platform that is firm and stable. This could be in direct response to something that your direct leader has asked of you, it could relate to organizational philosophy and core values, or it could be something birthed in your leadership heart. Wherever it comes from, you are responsible to bring clarity and focus so that you can clearly communicate it to the others whom you desire to raise up. If you don't have a clear blueprint and foundation on which to build, you cannot expect to develop leaders who will have what they need to continue with you on this journey.

> For we are God's fellow workers; you are God's field, you are God's building. According to the grace of God which was given to me, as a wise master builder I have laid the foundation, and another builds on it. But let each one take heed how he builds on it. For no other foundation can anyone lay than that which is laid, which is Jesus Christ.
> —1 Corinthians 3:9–11

One thing that is important is that the foundation carries the DNA of the end results that you are trying to accomplish in the leadership development. Everything built on the foundation should point back to the foundation so that the final product does not veer from the plan. When you develop leaders, the how and what may look different based on leadership styles, spiritual gifting, and personality, but the foundation should remain constant and throughout. A great leader will establish a clear foundation that infuses the "why" into other leaders. They will have what they need to use their specific callings to accomplish the why and everyone wins. They are empowered; the why remains; and you expand your influence.

## 2. Equip

This phase of building is all about providing the tools necessary for the individual to be equipped for long-term growth. Many people start well but fall short at different phases of growth. Putting a map or a blueprint in place with a clear discipleship growth track and organizational understanding is essential for expansion. If you have given a leader a strong foundation but don't give them the proper equipment with which to build, then the burden of loss is on you and not them.

Many times, we overlook the experience and training that we have learned and implemented over many years. We have a large toolbox that took many years to acquire, and we cannot expect others simply to be where we are. We must slow down our leadership and ensure that we are fully equipping those whom we are leading. To properly equip someone takes intentionality and process. We cannot simply give them a tool bag full of tools and think they have what they need for the task. A great leader walks with them through each step of the equipping before empowering them, skillfully teaching them how to use each tool and for what purposes.

> But in a great house there are not only vessels of gold and silver, but also of wood and clay, some for honor and some for dishonor. Therefore if anyone cleanses himself from the latter, he will be a vessel for honor, sanctified and useful for the Master, prepared for every good work.
> —*2 Timothy 2:20–21*

## 3. Empower

We understand that God has called all of us to minister with the gifts that He has placed in our lives. Our biblical community is a great place to be empowered to discover, grow, and minister with the gifts God has given each one. As leaders, this is one of the most important core values. If we spend all our time training, managing, and teaching our leaders but we never transition to empowering them, then our labor is in vain. Empowerment should be a welcome step in leadership development if we have done a good job of establishing and equipping.

Most people are capable of much more than the average leader gives them credit for. We should do everything possible to empower them with the gifts that God has placed inside of them. Many times, this can be the most difficult part of leadership. Sometimes it feels like handing over your baby to someone else. You have labored and led that thing for a season, and now you must let it go so that someone else can take it on. It's hard to see someone else taking over something that you have invested so much time, energy, and love into, but this is essential if we are going to raise up leaders to help us accomplish our vision.

No, they will not do it exactly as you would do it. Yes, they will make mistakes and fail. This is where relationship comes in. You must continue to lead them from more of a coaching perspective and less of that of a teammate. Coaches lead from the sidelines. The best coaches are the ones who find ways to empower their players to their full potential. Micromanagement is not an option if you're going to really empower people. Leaders who control will frustrate others and only be able to do so much before they burn out themselves.

Empowerment requires the skills to allow people to grow into their role with your accountable oversight and verification. You have to learn to let go and trust that the leader you have equipped will succeed and truly put into practice the gifts God has given them. At the end of the day, none of us is in ultimate control anyway. Remember that we are accountable to God and this is His show. If you don't learn to empower others, then you are not trusting God with His leaders.

*As each one has received a gift, minister it to one another, as good stewards of the manifold grace of God. If anyone speaks, let him speak as the oracles of God. If anyone ministers, let him do it as with the ability which God supplies, that in all things God may be glorified through Jesus Christ, to whom belong the glory and the dominion forever and ever. Amen.*

**—1 Peter 4:10–11**

## 4. Expand

Many leaders hit a certain lid in the growth and development of the organization portion of their ministry. This is a very critical time that can allow the organization to push through to the next level, crest and become stagnant, or even digress and go backward. Many leaders are willing to do what is necessary at this point, but they simply don't know what to do. It's crucial to help coach leaders to navigate well through this season and expand to the next season of ministry.

Many times, we stunt other's leadership potential because we hover over them and don't fully release them so that their ministry can expand. There are many reasons for this, but we must fight against those reasons and allow our investment to pay dividends.

The greatest example of empowerment and expansion can be seen when Christ released us into the world to make disciples. We see many examples of the "what" and "how" this has been accomplished, but the "why" is very clear. When we allow God to work in people's lives as we invest in them, He will expand His kingdom for His glory.

> But you shall receive power when the Holy Spirit has come upon you; and you shall be witnesses to Me in Jerusalem, and in all Judea and Samaria, and to the end of the earth.
>
> —*Acts 1:8*

> And Jesus came and spoke to them, saying, "All authority has been given to Me in heaven and on earth. Go there-

*fore and make disciples of all the nations, baptizing them in the name of the Father and of the Son and of the Holy Spirit, teaching them to observe all things that I have commanded you; and lo, I am with you always, even to the end of the age." Amen.*

**—Matthew 28:18-20**

## 5. Encourage

As a developer of leaders, one of the greatest things you can do is learn to simply be an encourager. Great leaders who have invested time, sweat, tears, and labor in the four Es of leadership already listed have a duty to become the best encourager they can be to those whom they have led.

It does not take much time and effort to be an encourager. If you lack this aspect of leadership development, you may miss an important opportunity to be a voice that helps others through a discouraging time. The verse below is an example of Paul encouraging the church at Corinth. He reminds them that their struggle and work is not in vain:

*Therefore, my beloved brethren, be steadfast, immovable, always abounding in the work of the Lord, knowing that your labor is not in vain in the Lord.*

**—1 Corinthians 15:58**

Don't ever miss a chance to encourage those whom you are leading!

APPENDIX B

# Journaling 101

The following information on journaling is used with permission from Rocky Fleming at www.Influencers.org.[28]

On your journey to intimacy with Christ, one thing that can greatly assist you is journaling. This is a foreign concept to most people. However, journaling can be a gift from God to you. Many times, we learn to internalize our thoughts, keeping them hidden in the deep recesses of our minds. Journaling is a way to help you get those issues out of your heart and onto the altar before God.

In this technological age of high-speed communication, written words have been lost. Today, most of our thoughts and reflections about life—if they even make it out of our heads—are condensed into brief digital formats, which are then deleted in cyberspace before they have a chance to sink into our consciousness. There is power in the written word on paper. God wants us to slow down, be still for a few moments with Him, and just like He instructed countless people from Moses to Paul, write down the revelations He gives us.

In the pages of this book is a lot of information for you to prayerfully navigate. We have included this simple form of journaling to help you put down on paper some key things that may be speaking the loudest to you. When you write things down, there is a tendency to remember more and create further action steps to implement the learning pieces. If you are going to invest the time to read this book, it would greatly benefit you to utilize journaling through the workbook section at the end of each chapter. If you are inspired to become an abiding leader of an Abiding Church, there will be much to process, and this method can help simplify this.

**STAR Journaling Exercise Template**

**#1 Scripture Read/Promise Given/Question Asked**

Read the verse and/or question and walk through the STAR/SPAR process. Pause and prayerfully meditate on what is being said, read, or asked.

_____

_____

_____

_____

_____

_____

## #2 Thought Conveyed/Promise Given

In this part, write down what this means to you so that you can clearly understand the question, scripture, thought, or promise. Make it personal to get the most out of it.

_____

_____

_____

_____

_____

_____

## #3 Application Made

How does this teaching apply to me right now? How does this apply to my leadership context?

_____

_____

_____

_____

_____

_____

## #4 Response Given

What can I do to immediately to apply this to my life? How should I respond/react to this promise or instruction? What are some long-term things to which I need to respond?

APPENDIX C

# Further Resources

The Journey is a nine- to twelve-month process, with most groups meeting every other week. It is divided into three main segments, called Enlightened, Enabled, and Expressing.

The Enlightened segment of the Journey is the foundation of the process. The step-by-step understanding of the four personal aspects of God (He Knows, He Cares, He Is Willing, and He Is Able) is designed to help the participant realize that God is a loving, caring, and intimate God who wants to involve Himself in every area of the participant's life. This new understanding should guide the participant to the goal of being willing to trust God with his life and prepares the way for the second segment of the Journey.

The Enabled segment of the Journey focuses on an abiding, intimate relationship with Jesus. This segment helps the participant understand how the Holy Spirit "enables" him to develop this new level of intimacy. He is guided through an understanding of the "fruit of the

Spirit" and how this fruit enables the use of the "gifts of the Spirit." This should help him to better understand his role and purpose in the work of God's kingdom. Above all else, the Enabled segment should guide the participant toward the goal of releasing control of his life and experiencing the joy of personal abandonment found in his abiding relationship with Jesus.

The Expressing segment of the Journey is the culmination of the Journey process. The principles of "Being a God Seeker," "Being a God Abider," and "Live It Out" are used as the guide to help the participant fully understand the entire Journey. He is introduced to the concept of servant leadership within his marriage, his family, and the world around him. He is challenged to grasp the concept of "blooming where he is planted" and how he is now ready to partner with God to influence his world in a supernatural way. At the end of the Journey, the participant is released to take the name "Influencer" and begin to bear fruit that lasts by expressing Christlike love to all those around him.

The Journey experience has three main components for each participant.

The first is his personal "treasure hunt," conducted during the days between sessions. This is the core of the Journey and the place where heart transformation takes place. This "treasure hunt" guides the participant toward the "Inner Chamber," where intimacy with Christ is discovered and experienced.

The second component is the one-on-one time between the guide and the participant. This individual time is critical to the participant's journey as the guide and the participant share their life stories.

The third component is the group sessions, designed for the group to discuss their journey and share discovered truth. Each session enhances the other two components and ties the Journey together.

This Journey process will lay a strong foundation that you can build upon as you pursue your long-term growth track.

Influencers is a ministry with the goal of guiding people into an intimate, abiding relationship with Jesus Christ. They accomplish this through Journey groups, who journey together for nine months, each desiring a closer proximity to the Father. Participants discover God in a most personal way through Scripture, journaling, group discussion, prayer, and study materials.

Jesus said, "I am the vine; you are the branches. If you remain in me and I in you, you will bear much fruit; apart from me you can do nothing" (John 15:5 NIV). For years, good Christian people have been striving to bear fruit for God. However, they have missed the part about "remaining in Him." Influencers helps people press the pause button in life, so that they can take time to seek Jesus and find renewed hope and purpose.

Thousands of people—and increasingly, women and married couples as well—have gone on this Journey worldwide, and thousands more are finding their way to this life-giving process. If you would like to know more about Influencers and the Journey and how to start a group in your city, go to the website at www.influencers.org.

## Other Resources

- *I'm a Catalyst* membership manual by Catalyst Church
- *Abiding at the Feet of Jesus: A Study of the Beatitudes* by Nate Sweeney
- *Abiding in Identity: Who I Am Because of Whose I Am* by Nate Sweeney
- *Journey to the Inner Chamber* by Rocky Fleming
- *Knowing Christ and Making Him Known* by Nate Sweeney
- *5-2-1 Leadership Planning*

REFERENCES

# Notes

1. Lloyd-Jones, D. Martin. *Studies in the Sermon on the Mount.* Reprint edition. Martino Fine Books, 2011.

2. Fleming, Rocky. "Journaling." *Influencers Global Ministries.* www.influencers.org/journaling.

3. Campolo, Tony. "Why the Church Is Important." May 1, 2007. *Christianity Today.* Quoted from *Letters to a Young Evangelical*, Basic Books, 2008. https://www.christianitytoday.com/ct/2007/mayw eb-only/118-22.0.html. Campolo loosely or inaccurately attributes the sentiment to Saint Augustine.

4. Barna, George. "Twentysomethings Struggle to Find Their Place in Christian Churches." September 24, 2003. *Millenials & Generations.* Barna Group, Inc. https://www.barna.com/research/twentysomethin gs-struggle-to-find-their-place-in-christian-churches.

5. Barna, "Twentysomethings Struggle to Find Their Place in Christian Churches."

6. McAdams, Andy. "The State of the Church in America—Key Statistics." January 31, 2010. *@djchuang*. http://djchuang.com/2010/churches-closing-and-pastors-leaving.

7. McAdams, "The State of the Church in America."

8. Though this is my personal assertion, others have made similar statements. See, for instance, John M. Fowler, *Ephesians: Chosen in Christ*, Review and Herald Publishing Association, 2005, p. 50.

9. Chambers, Sandra. "Billy Graham: A Faithful Witness." November 7, 2013. *Charisma News*. Charisma Media. https://www.charismanews.com/us/41684-billy-graham-a-faithful-witness.

10. "Transform." *Dictionary.com*. http://www.dictionary.com/browse/transform.

11. McAdams, "The State of the Church in America."

12. Crossway Bibles. ESV Study Bible. Kindle ed. Good News Publishers/Crossway Books, 2009, Kindle locations 119465–119468.

13. "Americans Spent $7.5 Bln. on Potato Chips in 2015." October 17, 2016. *Fresh Plaza*. http://www.freshplaza.com/article/165058/Americans-spent-7.5-bln-on-potato-chips-in-2015.

14. Forest Time. "How Much Do Americans Spend on Soft Drinks." September 29, 2017. *Classroom*. https://classroom.synonym.com/how-much-do-americans-spend-on-soft-drinks-12081634.html.

15. PTI. "Christians Hold Largest Percentage of Global Wealth: Report." January 14, 2015. *Financial Express.* https://www.financialexpress.com/industry/christians-hold-largest-percentage-of-global-wealth-report/30073.

16. Holmes, Mike. "What Would Happen If the Church Tithed?" Updated March 8, 2016. *Relevant.* https://relevantmagazine.com/love-and-money/what-would-happen-if-church-tithed.

17. Holmes, "What Would Happen If the Church Tithed?"

18. Holmes, "What Would Happen If the Church Tithed?"

19. Tatum, Malcolm. "What Is a Parachurch Organization?" Edited by Bronwyn Harris. January 14, 2018. *wiseGeek.* Conjecture Corporation. http://www.wisegeek.com/what-is-a-parachurch-organization.htm.

20. "What Percentage of Your Life Will You Spend at Work?" August 16, 2016. *ReviseSociology.* https://revisesociology.com/2016/08/16/percentage-life-work.

21. Tenney, Tommy. *The God Chasers: "My Soul Follows Hard After Thee."* Destiny Image Publishers, 1998.

22. Copeland, Larry. "Life Expectancy Hits Record High." October 9, 2014. *USA Today.* https://www.usatoday.com/story/news/nation/2014/10/08/us-life-expectancy-hits-record-high/16874039.

23. Booth, William. *The Pulse of a Nation: Sound*

*the Alarm*. Go to Nations Publishing, 2015.

24. Jillette, Penn. "Not Proselytize." YouTube video. November 18, 2009. In Justin Taylor, "How Much Do You Have to Hate Someone *Not* to Proselytize?" Gospel Coalition. https://www.thegospelcoalition.org/blogs/justin-taylor/how-much-do-you-have-to-hate-somebody-to-not-proselytize.

25. Thomas, R. L. "Paraklētos." *New American Standard Hebrew-Aramaic and Greek Dictionaries*. Updated edition. Foundation Publications, Inc., 1998.

26. Thomas, R. L. "Dunamis." *New American Standard Hebrew-Aramaic and Greek Dictionaries*. Updated edition. Foundation Publications, Inc., 1998.

27. "Culture." *Dictionary.com*. Dictionary.com. http://www.dictionary.com/browse/culture.

28. Fleming, "Journaling."

# About the Author

Nate Sweeney would be considered an average person, someone who loves his family, community, and church. The major factor that sets him apart is his passion to Know Christ and Make Him Known. This vision is at the forefront of Nate's daily focus and drives him to stay connected to Christ and share that relationship with others. Nate pursues this vision in his home with his wife, Monica, and their three kids.

Nate has served in many ministry capacities since he

graduated from Bible school in 1997. He is the directional leader of Catalyst Church in Bentonville, Arkansas. Nate is also the founder and directional leader of The Abiding Network, and he sits on the Influencers Ministry global board as a church relations leader.

Nate speaks with experience, as he has led his church to be transformed into an Abiding Church, and his role has become supported by the great leaders who have been raised up in this church. At the time of this publishing, Nate has mentored, coached, and helped disciple hundreds of church leaders nationally.

It is evident, through Nate's ministry, that people are challenged to daily experience God and grow in their relationship with Him, while discovering what He has called them to do in life and share His love in practical ways.

# About Sermon To Book

SermonToBook.com began with a simple belief: that sermons should be touching lives, *not* collecting dust. That's why we turn sermons into high-quality books that are accessible to people all over the globe.

Turning your sermon series into a book exposes more people to God's Word, better equips you for counseling, accelerates future sermon prep, adds credibility to your ministry, and even helps make ends meet during tight times.

John 21:25 tells us that the world itself couldn't contain the books that would be written about the work of Jesus Christ. Our mission is to try anyway. Because in heaven, there will no longer be a need for sermons or books. Our time is now.

If God so leads you, we'd love to work with you on your sermon or sermon series.

Visit www.sermontobook.com to learn more.

Made in United States
Orlando, FL
10 August 2023

35970607R00143